Paleo Diet for Beginners: Lose Weight and Get Healthy

ABOUT THE AUTHOR

The goal of "Lady Pannana" Publishing Company is to provide you with easy-to-cook, authentic, and tasty recipes.

To increase your health, energy, and well-being, Lady Pannana cookbooks bring together the best of international cuisines and teach you how to cook them in the comfort of your own home.

From special diets to international treats, pick up a cookbook today and lose yourself in a whole new world of possibilities.

No mealtime should be boring, so go ahead and treat yourself!

Browse our catalog of titles and don't forget to tell us what you think about our books. We want to create a better experience for our readers. Your voice, your opinion, and your input only serve to ensure that the next time you pick up a Lady Pannana Publishing Title, it will be better than the last!

Medical Disclaimer

Introduction

I want to thank you and congratulate you for purchasing the book *"Paleo Diet: Paleo Diet for Beginners: Lose Weight And Get Healthy"*.

This book has actionable information on how to lose weight and get healthy by following the Paleo diet.

We can all agree that while there are major scientific breakthroughs on various facets of human life, the general population is struggling with some things that they really shouldn't be struggling with. For instance, obesity seems to be a worldwide problem and if the statistics are anything to go by, more and more people seem to be becoming obese or overweight.

Why is that so? Can't we just eat the right foods and avoid the wrong foods?

Well, while there are many theories behind that, there is a striking correlation between obesity and economic development. More precisely, developed nations seem to be struggling more than those that are still developing. What could be the problem? What's wrong with economic development and industrialization?

Simple: what the masses are consuming. With economic development comes more reliance on store bought ingredients and foods. What you may not know is that these ingredients have gone through genetic engineering, processing and much, much more that changes the original (natural ingredient) to some extent. This is bad for your body as these foods tend to have traces of substances that the body is not yet fully evolved to metabolize effectively. While the body does its best to metabolize some of these, most times the process is not efficient and it leaves behind toxic waste that is harmful for the body in the long term. The accumulation of this toxic waste in the body is what often times causes inflammation and fat accumulation (especially around the belly area). This perhaps explains why our modern society is plagued with so many diseases.

To reverse this toxic buildup that leads to obesity you have to choose a diet containing ingredients in their natural form or as close to their natural form as possible, as this is what the human body evolved for thousands of years to metabolize. This is the crux of the Paleolithic diet and this book will show you exactly what the Paleo diet is all about including:

- How it works

- How it came into being

- The foods you should eat while on the Paleo diet

- Foods you should avoid while on the Paleo diet

- The benefits you stand to derive when you follow the Paleo diet

- How to pair the Paleo diet with exercise

- Mistakes you should avoid while on the diet and much, much more!

By following this book, you will understand how the Paleolithic man was able to remain healthy, agile and fit so that you can model your life like his to stave off various health problems. Let's begin.

Thanks again for purchasing this book. I hope you enjoy it!

Table of Contents

Introduction 6

The Paleo Diet: A Comprehensive Background 14

Foods to Eat 17

Foods Not to Eat 31

Top 20 Foods on The Paleo Diet 38

A Journey through History: Paleo Diet History 48

Latest Evidence on Paleo Effectiveness 50

What's in it For You? The Benefits of the Paleo diet .53

Getting Started on the Paleo Diet 69

How to Make Your Paleo Diet a Success 74

Mistakes to Avoid When on the Paleo Diet 98

Why the Paleo Diet is Not Working for You 102

4-Week Workout Plan 109

Paleo for Bodybuilders and Athletes 118

How Much Macro-Nutrients do You Need? 121

4-Week Meal Plan 125

Week 1 125

Day 1 125

Day 2 126

Day 3 127

Day 4 128

Day 5 129

Day 6 130

Day 7 131

Week 2 133

Day 1 133

Day 2 134

Day 3 134

Day 4 135

Day 5 136

Day 6 137

Day 7 137

Week 3 139

Day 1 139

Day 2 140

Day 3 141

Day 4 141

Day 5 142

Day 6 144

Day 7 145

Week 4 146

Day 1 146

Day 2 147

Day 3..148

Day 4..149

Day 5..150

Day 6 151

Day 7 153

Delicious Paleo Recipes 155

Breakfast Recipes...155

Lunch Recipes...197

For Cajun Seasoning 213

Dinner Recipes 241

Paleo Snack Recipes...292

Paleo Dessert Recipes 326

Conclusion..356

The Paleo Diet: A Comprehensive Background

Since this is a beginners' guide, we will start by building a strong understanding of what the diet is all about.

What is it?

The word Paleo diet comes from "Paleolithic Diet," a term used to refer to a dietary lifestyle that is rapidly becoming popular globally. The diet, considered to reflect what our ancestors ate, has been attributed to many benefits. Among them are boosting energy levels, weight loss and healing ailments linked to poor dietary lifestyles. The premise of the diet is simple; if the Paleolithic man didn't eat something, don't eat it either and if he ate something, you are free to eat it as well.

During the caveman's era, our ancestors were thought to only eat game or wild meat, nuts, poultry, seafood and fruits such as berries. Grains and dairy were unheard of during those days, as humans had not yet started practicing agriculture.

Interestingly, the caveman didn't suffer from health problems that we have today like cancer and diabetes.

This shows there was something about the Paleolithic way of life that kept these health complications away.

What could that be? Well, while there might be many contributing factors, one of the things that stands out is the fact that food did not go through genetic modification to increase yield. There was no need for processing to enhance shelf life or add value and there was no need to domesticate animals or practice agriculture since food was in plenty. This means the food was very natural and free from insecticides, pesticides and other harmful chemicals since it existed in nature without the Paleolithic man's interference/input. This worked in his favor, as the body had evolved for hundreds of thousands of years until it was fully capable of utilizing the various components in such foods. As such, the toxic waste I mentioned earlier was nonexistent and as such, weight problems hardly existed.

Agriculture (planting various crops and domestication) didn't start until around 10,000 years ago. This is the time that humans started growing grains and started consuming dairy. Then fast forward to the 1700s and 1800s when the industrial revolution started. This marked the beginning of a series of events that saw more changes being done to food production to increase yield, increase resistance and quicken maturity. The use of pesticides, insecticides, fertilizers, fungicides and other substances increased. And after harvesting, processing of food started taking place. Some substances are now added to food to increase shelf life, to change color, to change taste and any other number of reasons. And since then, the trend has not stopped: we consume more factory-made or modified foods than ever before. And what has been the result? Well, the result has been a wide array of health complications that have plagued our society like never before because our bodies have not yet evolved to a point of fully metabolizing the foods that we eat these days. In fact, our body treats some of these foods as toxins, which explains why we face the health complications that we have these days. The Paleo diet seeks to eliminate the modern foods that are likely to cause various health problems and instead focuses on eating what our Paleolithic ancestors ate. Eliminating foods like refined sugar, dairy, grains, cereals, salt and replacing them with natural foods like grass fed meat, olive oil, nuts, seeds, vegetables and fruits.

Let's take it further by discussing the specific foods you are allowed to eat and those you are not allowed to eat while on the Paleo diet.

Foods to Eat

1. Paleo diet meats

By definition, almost all meats fall in the Paleo diet i.e. game meat, poultry, red meat and white meat. The rule of the thumb is to buy fresh meats rather than those that have been marinated, batter-coated or breaded. Also, choose meat from pastured animals to avoid toxins associated with non-organically raised animals e.g. given antibiotics.

Enjoy organic meats such as:

- Bison (bison jerky, bison sirloin, bison steaks, etc.)

- Buffalo

- Chicken (chicken breast, chicken thighs, chicken wings, eggs, etc.)

- Elk

- Emu

- Goat

- Goose

- Beef (steak, ground beef, New York steak, chuck steak, beef jerky, etc.)

- Kangaroo

- Lamb (lamb chops, lamb rack, etc.)

- Ostrich

- Pheasant

- Pork (bacon, pork chops, pork tenderloin, etc.)

- Poultry

- Quail

- Rabbit

- Rattlesnake

- Turkey

- Turtle

- Veal (lean veal)

- Venison

- Wild boar

2. Paleo diet fish and shellfish

Fish are one of the most important foods in the Paleo diet, and they are packed with great nutrients such as omega 3 fatty acids. The following fish and seafood are top picks for the Paleo diet:

- Bass
- Clams
- Crab
- Crawfish
- Crayfish
- Halibut
- Lobster
- Mackerel
- Mussels
- Oysters
- Red snapper
- Salmon
- Sardines
- Scallops

- Shark

- Shrimp

- Sunfish

- Swordfish

- Tilapia

- Trout

- Tuna

3. Paleo diet oils and fats

Contrary to the common belief that reducing fat intake facilitates weight loss, this has proven not to be the case for a number of reasons. First, fats tend to be very satiating compared to carbohydrates, which means that if you eat them, you won't have the urge to eat as often as if you had eaten carbohydrates. This essentially means you end up consuming less calories. That's not all; eating more fats and oils means that you will effectively eat less carbohydrates. As a result, you reduce your insulin production. Having high levels of insulin hormone in the body has been shown to put the body in a state of fat storage.. In fact, high insulin levels favor a process referred to as glycolysis i.e. fat creation. However, if you eat fewer carbohydrates, you end up producing lower levels of insulin, which in turn helps you to stop storing fats.

The following is a list of some of the best Paleo fats and oils for additional energy when trying to lose weight:

- Avocado oil

- Coconut oil

- Macadamia oil

- Olive oil

4. Veggies

When it comes to veggies, the list is endless. All you need is to choose colored non-starchy veggies such as kales and tomatoes. The rule of the thumb is to eat leafy green veggies and whole fruits rather than starchy veggies, fruit juices and processed salads that contain added sugars. Eat any of these food groups as long as they are organically grown or unprocessed, and contain no added sweeteners or chemicals.

Here are a few you should enjoy:

- Asparagus

- Broccoli

- Brussels sprouts

- Cabbage

- Carrots

- Cauliflower

- Celery

- Collard greens

- Eggplant

- Green onion

- Kale

- Parsley

- Peppers

- Spinach

- Tomatoes

In addition to the above you are also free to eat the following root vegetables:

- Artichokes

- Beets

- Carrots

- Cassava

- Parsnips

- Radish

- Rutabaga

- Sweet potatoes

- Turnips

- Yams

Squashes are also a great addition to the diet:

- Acorn squash

- Buttercup squash

- Butternut squash

- Pumpkin

- Spaghetti squash

- Yellow crookneck squash

- Yellow summer squash

- Zucchini

Mushrooms are also in this category. Therefore, feel free to eat:

- Button mushroom

- Chantarelle mushroom

- Crimini mushroom

- Morel mushroom

- Oyster mushroom

- Porcini mushroom

- Portabello mushroom

- Shiitake mushroom

5. Paleo diet fruits

Fruits are delicious and double up as a source of a wide range of nutrients. However, fruits tend to be rich in fructose, which is still sugar. Therefore, it is advisable to cut back on your fruit intake if you are trying to lose weight on a Paleo diet. That said; feel free to indulge in a serving or two of fruit per day. Here is a list of Paleo-approved fruits:

- Apples

- Avocado

- Bananas

- Blackberries

- Blueberries

- Cantaloupe

- Figs

- Grapes

- Guava

- Lemon

- Lime

- Lychee

- Mango

- Oranges

- Papaya

- Peaches

- Pineapple

- Plums

- Raspberries

- Strawberries

- Tangerines

- Watermelon

6. Paleo diet nuts

These are a good choice for snacks as they contain high quantities of unsaturated fats that are heart-healthy. However, due to being high in calories, you should moderate the intake of nuts to a handful a day. Also, avoid those honey-roasted or candied and heavily salted nuts. You can choose varieties of seeds and nuts from these suggestions:

- Almonds

- Cashews

- Hazelnuts

- Macadamia nuts

- Pecans

- Pine nuts

- Pumpkin seeds

- Sunflower seeds

- Walnuts

Note: Since peanuts are not technically a type of nut, they do not make it onto the Paleo list.

7. Natural spices and herbs

Most Paleo foods do not require added preservatives, and can be stored through traditional methods such as freezing, canning, salting, smoking and fermentation. However if spices are your thing, go for those with no additives such as chili hot peppers, cinnamon and other natural sweeteners.

Here is the full list:

- Basil

- Bay leaves

- Black pepper

- Chilies
- Chives
- Cinnamon
- Cloves
- Coriander (fresh and seeds)
- Cumin
- Dill
- Fennel seeds
- Fresh parsley
- Garlic
- Horseradish
- Hot peppers
- Lavender
- Mint
- Nutmeg
- Nutmeg
- Onions
- Rosemary

- Salt

- Smoked paprika

- Star anise

- Tarragon

- Thyme

- Vanilla

Foods Not to Eat

The following list is a comprehensive collection of all the foods you should try to avoid while on the Paleo diet to lose weight. Chances are you will find it hard to keep yourself from eating these in the beginning, but once you get the hang of it, it becomes much easier.

Moreover, you are also likely to find much better substitutes for these foods.

Dairy

- Cheese

- Cottage cheese

- Cream cheese

- Dairy spreads

- Frozen yogurt

- Ice cream

- Milk (low-fat milk, 2% milk, whole milk, powdered milk, ice milk, etc.)

- Non-fat dairy creamer

- Pudding

- Yogurt

Fruit Juices and Soft Drinks

These are high in sugar and can upset your quest to losing weight, so stay away from them. In fact, soft drinks such as coke are full of high fructose corn syrup and sugar, and are therefore not Paleo friendly. Some of the juices and soft drinks to avoid include:

- Apple juice

- Coke

- Fanta

- Grape juice

- Mango juice

- Monster energy drink

- Mountain Dew

- Orange juice

- Pepsi

- Red bull

- Sprite

- Strawberry juice

Grains

Avoid anything that typically has grains in it. These include rice, wheat, barley and oats along with products that come from them such as crackers, bagels, cereal, pasta, granola bars and bread. Simply avoid every type of food that has grains in it, whether whole-grain, processed grains or whatever kind of grains you come across. Instead, try almond or coconut flour; these are low carb, high fiber, and protein rich.

Here is a list of some grains to avoid:

- Bread

- Cereals

- Corn

- Corn syrup (high-fructose corn syrup)

- Crackers

- Cream of wheat

- English muffins

- Hash browns

- Lasagna

- Oatmeal

- Pancakes

- Pasta

- Sandwiches

- Toast

- Wheat

- Wheat Thins

Legumes

Here are the ones you should stay away from:

Beans

- Adzuki beans

- Black beans

- Broad beans

- Fava beans

- Garbanzo beans

- Green beans

- Horse beans

- Kidney beans

- Lima beans

- Navy beans

- Pinto beans
- Red beans
- String beans
- White beans

Peas

- Black-eyed peas
- Chickpeas
- Snow peas
- Sugar snap peas

Peanuts

- All soybean products and derivatives
- Lentils
- Mesquite
- Miso
- Peanut butter
- Soybeans
- Tofu

Artificial sweeteners

By definition, no artificial sweeteners are included in the Paleo diet. If you want to sweeten your foods, use maple syrup, honey, or Stevia instead.

Fatty meats, snacks, and salty foods

Avoid processed foods, those with too much salt, or other quick snacks that come in a packaged form. For example, if you want to eat meat, just go for some steak, but stay away from these fatty foods:

- Chips

- Cookies

- French fries

- Hot dogs

- Ketchup

- Pastries

- Pretzels

- Wheat Thins

Alcohol

Alcohol is a gluten product and for this reason is not included in the Paleo diet. This includes, but is not limited to:

- Alcohol and mixers

- Beer

- Rum

- Tequila

- Vodka

- Whiskey

The list of foods to eat and those to avoid is undoubtedly long. What you might be wondering is; are there some foods that you should make the center of your diet to derive the most benefits? We will discuss up to 20 foods that you should strive to include in your diet to help you get started.

Top 20 Foods on The Paleo Diet

1. Coconut Oil

Coconut is a potent source of lauric acid, a heart healthy fatty acid that has antiviral and anti-bacterial properties. Due to these factors, coconut oil is a great choice for boosting the immune system through destruction of bacteria and viruses.

More precisely, if you are trying to lose weight, coconut oil can help burn fat and clean up the body, as it boosts its ability to process long chain fatty acids. The Lauric acid in the coconut oil also increases the amount of lauric acid in breast milk. This powerful anti-microbial fatty acid can be very effective in improving the immune system in babies and even fetuses when they are in the womb. The acid, once it reaches the cells, is converted into mono-laurin, a substance that can treat various viruses.

2. Chicken

Chicken is a very common food for most diet plans, the Paleo diet included, and for several reasons; it is easy to prepare, it's versatile and can suit hundreds of recipes for delicious meals.

Chicken is high in protein and is best eaten from free-range or organic sources, similar to what the caveman ate. The meat from chicken has good amounts of magnesium, vitamin B-6 and vitamin B-12 that boost energy levels.

3. Broccoli

This very nutrient-dense food is high in fiber, a substance that keeps the digestive system working properly.

Broccoli is also rich in vitamin C and antioxidants, which strengthen the immune system and fight off colds and the flu. Actually, a cup of broccoli has about 135 percent of the daily nutritional requirement for vitamin C.

4. Spinach

This super food has the highest nutrient level regardless of the diet plan you are on. It's packed with minerals like potassium and magnesium, fiber, and phytonutrients and vitamins like A and C; all of which improve digestion and create a broad nutritional profile. For instance, magnesium is important in preventing osteoporosis and cardiovascular infections, while potassium is good for blood sugar level and heart health.

Spinach is also high in phytonutrients and antioxidants that enable the body to fight free radicals. It offers you adequate energy, stabilize the blood glucose and enhance your general wellbeing.

Try eating spinach when fresh and avoid frozen, as fresh spinach has higher heart and anti-cancer benefits.

5. Free-range eggs

Eggs are high in high quality protein, minerals and vitamins A, B and B-6. Eggs often make a big part of the breakfast meal, but can also be eaten throughout the entire day.

In order to eat eggs like the Paleolithic man, you need to eat the entire egg; white and yolk. The egg yolk is rich in minerals and omega-3s that can benefit your body.

Ensure you eat from free-range chicken, as they are rich in omega-3 fatty acids, vitamin D and amino acids. These minerals are important for hormone regulation, healthy skin and hair. Also, look for dark-orange yoked eggs, as they are higher in omega 3, which helps facilitate fat loss. Eggs offer the most usable or easy to metabolize protein compared to meats.

6. Wild-caught salmon

This pricey seafood is packed with proteins, omega 3 fatty acids, minerals and vitamins. The omega 3 in wild-caught salmon is effective for inflammation, while the protein is a building block for muscles. Try eating the deep reddish orange salmon at least every 3 days to ensure you get potassium and vitamins like B-6 and B-12.

7. Asparagus

This rare food is rich in fiber, which facilitates digestion, and can be eaten cooked or raw due to its amazing taste. It's also rich in minerals and vitamins and can serve as a good complement to meat that has no fiber. Asparagus can also be easily prepared through grilling and streaming methods, and tastes delicious.

8. Watermelon

This fruit has high concentration of lycopene and potassium, which are suitable for heart health. Lycopene also helps the body to fight cancerous cells.

9. Kale

Kale, just like spinach, is one of the healthiest veggies. They contain phytonutrients, or antioxidants, which help the body to fight inflammation. Kale is also rich in vitamin A, B-6, C and calcium, which help replace dairy products that you miss out on the Paleo diet.

When eating veggies like kale, balance them out with organic meats to ensure you get adequate nutrients in your full meal.

Tip: You can cook kale to higher temperatures than spinach, as it doesn't wilt or shrink when cooked.

10. Almonds

The good thing about these nuts is that they are satiating and can be paired with different dishes. The fact that they are rich in proteins and fiber enables them to enhance satiety. The fiber and magnesium in almonds also enhances digestion.

You can easily substitute gluten or wheat flour with almond floor when you crave for baked goods.

Tip: The fiber in almonds can't be overcooked, and the calcium level from a cup of almonds is around 25 percent of the average daily requirement.

11. Blueberries

This super food is rich in antioxidants (known as anthocyanins) that come straight from nature. These antioxidants can greatly help you to fight free radicals in the body.

You can use these to fight brain disorders such as dementia and Alzheimer's disease. The berries are also good at rehabilitating brain function.

Tip: Look for those deep blue-colored blueberries, as they have high antioxidant properties.

12. Beets

Beets have a nutrient referred to as betalains, which is rare in other vegetables. This substance has strong antioxidant properties that can detox the body more effectively that most veggies. That's not all; beets are rich in fiber, iron, calcium and vitamin C.

Tip: Ensure that you buy fresh beets and then prepare them by steaming or grilling in order to soften them. Do not buy pickled beets in jars or salad bars, as they don't offer many benefits.

13. Lean beef

During the Paleolithic times, humans ate a lot of meat. However, keep in mind that beef is allowed only if it's lean cuts from organic or grass fed cattle. Organic meat is recommended since it is not treated with chemicals, antibiotics or hormones that can be toxic to the body.

Lean beef has low saturated fats and high quality protein. The protein is an important building block for strong muscles and also improves satiety.

Note: Remember that meat has no fiber so make sure to eat it together with veggies.

14. Cucumber

These can serve as a good snack or a side dish. They have high water content, which makes them satiating and helps them to keep your body hydrated.

That's not all; it's also high in minerals like magnesium and vitamins, and has excellent anti-cancer and detox effects. It can be blended into a smoothie to quench your thirst.

Tip: You should buy organic cucumber and include its peels in your meal for the maximum nutritional value.

15. Tomato

These are rich in lycopene, an antioxidant, which can help you to fight cancer, prevent heart disease, facilitate weight loss, and fight inflammation. Tomatoes also offer high amounts of vitamin C, which is good for the immune system, and calcium, which supports healthy teeth and bones.

Tip: You can either cook tomatoes or eat them raw (the choice is yours). However, cooked tomatoes are said to be healthier.

16. Celery

Celery is good for the body because it acts a diuretic; in other words, it helps the body get rid of excess fluids and toxins. It is also high in vitamin A, B-6 and C as well as fiber, which can help you to boost digestion.

This hydrating vegetable is a perfect ingredient for green smoothies and is also great in soups. Celery can also be a great snack that you can carry to your office or anywhere else.

17. Turkey

Our Paleolithic ancestors hunted for all sorts of wild animals, including turkey. That's why turkey is one of the key ingredients you should include in your diet.

Though you might not get wild turkey, reach for a whole roasted turkey and not turkey cold cuts if you want maximum benefits. This is because turkey breast in the form of cold cuts might have absorbed sodium and nitrates during processing, chemicals that are toxic to the body.

A roasted turkey breast has high quality protein, minerals like iron and vitamin C.

Turkey can serve as a replacement for chicken as it has similar nutritional values.

18. Grapefruit

The fruit is rich in vitamin C, which can help you remain energized throughout the day, and has metabolism-boosting properties. Grapefruit also contains vitamin A, B 6 and magnesium. That's not all, grapefruit can also fight cancer and regulate cholesterol towards healthy levels. This is good news given that some Paleo diet foods contain cholesterol.

You can start off your morning with a healthy bite of grapefruit to sustain you throughout the day. The fruit can also replace those sweet snacks and make you fuller for longer.

19. Apple

Apples are high in fiber and antioxidants that help you fight cancer and other degenerative diseases, among them Alzheimer's. Apples are handy since they are satiating (because they are rich in pectin, which is a dietary fiber) and thus are good snack options.

They are rich in vitamin C and potassium, which help boost energy levels. Reach for organic ones to avoid chemicals such as pesticides.

20. Avocado

Avocados are full of healthy fats and potassium. More precisely, a cup of avocado has 14 grams of monounsaturated fats, and 27 percent of the average daily potassium needs. The fats coupled with the high fiber content can help keep you full for longer since they enhance satiety and keep cravings at bay. Avocadoes are also high in vitamins B6 and vitamin C.

Other super foods that you should introduce into your life to help you succeed in your quest to following a Paleo lifestyle include the following:

- Kiwi fruit

- Cherries

- Dark chocolate

- Garlic

Now that you know some of the foods you should eat and those you should avoid, the next thing we will discuss is a brief history of how the diet came into being.

A Journey through History: Paleo Diet History

Before the term 'Paleo' was even developed, a man by the name of Joseph Knowles went to live in the forest for 2 months in 1913. During his 2-month stay in the wilderness, he researched what it was like to live like a hunter and gatherer, or like our ancestors who lived during the Stone Age.

The man had to survive in the forest only on the food available in his territory, most of them being fruits and vegetables. At the end of his experiment, he apparently informed everyone that the new diet had transformed him into a healthy and strong man.

Joseph formulated the idea that the sudden urbanization of the US had played a part in deviation from traditional living. The deviation, he predicted, was responsible for reduced health and common lifestyle problems.

Later, the term Paleo diet was developed by a gastroenterologist known as Walter L. Voegtlin through his book published in 1975, "The Stone Age Diet". It was in this book that human beings were described as naturally carnivorous, a diet that could keep them as healthy and strong as the ancestral man. The doctor believed that since our genetic blueprint comes directly from the Paleolithic man, we should only eat the Paleo diet in order to remain healthy and active.

In addition, he demonstrated how human beings evolved into carnivores based on biology, meaning that our physical shape should dictate the types of food to eat. The ancient man hunted for game and therefore mostly ate meat, as well as fruits and vegetables that were available in the forest. These foods are also easily absorbed and are more beneficial compared to a processed and sugary diet.

During the 1990s more people endorsed the diet, and it gained momentum into the 21st century. It is now the healthiest and purest diet, as modern research has proven. Currently, over 3 million Americans are said to be on the Paleo diet.

Let's see what scientists are currently saying about Paleo.

Latest Evidence on Paleo Effectiveness

While most of diets haven't been previously tested in the long term or experimented through medical literature, the Paleo diet has definitely attracted researchers who have begun to dig more into it.

At first, a 2015 review by the British Dietetic Association done to ascertain Paleolithic nutrition classified Paleo as a dangerous celebrity-endorsed diet. However, one year later, evidence on the benefits of Paleo has cleared the idea that Paleo was among the most dangerous diets and instead found that it hadn't been adequately tested during the review. Experimental studies have corroborated that the fact that the Paleo diet is superior to diabetic diets, and the "USDA My Plate" diet that seeks to introduce the nutrients that lack in US diets.

The latest evidence, which corroborates other scientific studies, shows that Paleo is a superior, low carb, high fat diet that can facilitate weight loss and bring about other therapeutic health benefits. For instance, a study by Lindeberg S, et al shows that the Paleo diet can boost glucose tolerance more effectively compared to the Mediterranean diet; particularly in people suffering from ischemic heart disease. The research involved 29 men suffering from high blood sugar and heart disease who adapted the Paleo diet without calorie restrictions. After about 12 weeks, the participants were evaluated in terms of insulin levels, weight, glucose tolerance and their waist circumference. In the findings, participants on the Paleo diet had great improvement on glucose tolerance and insulin levels. Glucose tolerance is a test that measures how long it takes for glucose to be cleared from the bloodstream.

On weight loss, participants on Paleo were able to lose around 11 pounds compared to a control group that only lost 8 pounds. The main difference was seen in waist circumference; the Paleo group had reduced by 5.6 cm while the control group only managed 2.9cm. All patients in the Paleo group ended up with normal blood glucose levels and were able to eat 450 fewer calories per day without the need to monitor food portions. At the conclusion of the study, the Paleo diet was considered to be superior in glycemic index control and weight loss compared to Paleo-like diets e.g. Mediterranean diet.

A related study by Jonsson T, et al. was conducted to establish the cardiovascular benefits of the Paleo diet on patients who suffered from type II diabetes. In the study, 13 diabetic participants on the Paleo diet were able to lose 6.6 pounds more than the control group within 3 months. The group also lost 4 cm more of their waist circumference on Paleo compared to those on diabetic diets. HDL, the good cholesterol, increased by 3 mg/dL in the Paleo group and triglycerides went down by 35 mg/dL when compared to the control group. The study confirms that Paleo is effective in both weight loss and cardiovascular improvements compared to the Diabetes diet.

While all these studies have endorsed the diet, Paleo is still somehow cited as a very difficult diet to follow because it requires dieters to avoid all grains, legumes and dairy products, which are part of a modern US diet.

Some of these include the following: one, the belief that any diet that bans whole food groups is 'suspicious' since there has been scientific evidence that legumes and whole grains can be healthy; two, the attribution of red meat to health risks, such as bowel cancer; and three, the belief that the modern Paleo diet is inconsistent with what our ancestors ate.

Well, quite a challenge convincing everyone, it seems! But to help you to understand all the goodness that the Paleo diet has to offer, let's discuss the specific benefits that the Paleo diet can bring you in detail.

What's in it For You? The Benefits of the Paleo diet

1. Accelerated weight loss

By just switching to a Paleo diet and doing nothing else, you will effectively be able to shed off a few pounds. What's the explanation for that weight loss?

Well, for starters, organic and unprocessed foods such as fatty fish, veggies, fruits, and lean meats do not add unnecessary calories to the body. These foods offer nutrients that support healthy cell function and an accelerated metabolism to burn off fat. By following a Paleo diet, you can lose weight fast within a few weeks, especially with moderate exercise routines like walking and occasional jogging (the Paleo man was not lazy—he spent his days hunting and gathering).

Secondly, the diet is rich in satiating foods, which help reduce appetite and unhealthy snacking. Frequent hunger and cravings can easily make you have a hard time sticking to the diet as a beginner. The Paleo diet incorporates a sufficient amount of healthy fats like olive and coconut oil that promote satiety and curb unnecessary cravings. You also get to eat an ample amount of fruits and vegetables, which tend to be high in fiber. This high fiber concentration can help boost satiety, as it's very filling. Fiber is important in absorbing water and takes up a lot of space in the stomach, which effectively means you will have less space for food. And when you eat less, this means you will end up creating the much needed calorie deficit that can help you to lose weight. The recommended amount of fiber per day is 25-35 grams so make sure to eat lots of fruits and vegetables to maximize your fiber consumption.

Since the various ingredients in this diet keep you full a lot of the time, you will hardly experience diet crashes and aren't "forced to cheat", as you only eat when hungry.

2. Boosts your health

Healthy and unprocessed foods can strengthen your immune system and thus minimize risk of hypertension, stroke or heart disease.

How do these foods do that? Here are some good examples:

- Fruits and veggies are rich in vitamin C, which strengthens blood vessels.

- Dark green veggies are rich in antioxidants and phytonutrients, which kill free radicals that are correlated to diseases like cancer.

- Fruits and veggies have good bacteria or probiotics, which help gut health and immunity.

- And, healthy fats from olive oil, avocados and nuts can lower blood cholesterol, which in turn boosts your hearth health.

In addition to that, you don't eat junk food or foods that have empty calories while on the Paleo diet. This is because the diet focuses predominantly on nutrient dense whole foods as opposed to processed foods. Cutting on processed food makes you feel better with sustained energy, without sugar crashes.

Since every calorie or food you consume serves a purpose, you can then transform your body positively. So there's no need to count calories anymore as there are no rigid rules on how much food you should eat; what's important is to eat like the Paleolithic man (which is healthy). You no longer have to limit yourself anymore and thus your brain cannot revolt against you or reject the diet plan (because of low will power).

3. Helps promote thyroid function

The thyroid is as a butterfly-shaped gland that sits low on the front of the neck, just slightly below the Adams apple. The main role of thyroid gland is to facilitate the synthesis, storage and release of thyroid hormones into the blood.

The brain regulates the thyroid hormone through the thyroid gland, pituitary gland and hypothalamus.

If you have too little thyroid hormone in the blood, this may cause your body functions to slow down, a condition that is referred to as hypothyroidism. When you have excess thyroid hormone in the blood, this results in the speeding up of bodily functions, i.e. hyperthyroidism. Weight gain is one of the main symptoms linked to thyroid problems, regardless of whether the thyroid becomes over-reactive or under-reactive.

Research shows that most of the factors that trigger thyroid problems are also linked to weight gain, such as a high-carb diet, insufficient protein consumption, unhealthy fats, and a lack of essential nutrients. Thus, the key to healthy thyroid function and controlled body weight is consuming healthier nutrients, reducing carbohydrate consumption, eating more protein, etc... Which is exactly what the Paleo diet is; high in protein (from grass fed beef, fish, poultry, seafood etc.) and nutrient rich (fruits are rich in nutrients such as zinc, copper, omega-3 fatty acids, vitamins A, B and D as well as selenium).

Note: Omega-3 fatty acids from wild caught fish or pastured eggs are vital in increasing response to thyroid hormones. You can obtain selenium by eating foods such as sunflower seeds, beef, Brazil nuts, salmon, mushrooms and onions.

Here a few tips to address thyroid problems with a Paleo lifestyle, which in turn helps control weight gain and related symptoms:

- *Limit sugary diet*

If you experience symptoms such as brain fog and crippling fatigue, your body may crave foods high in sugar and caffeine, which can burn the thyroid and destabilize your blood sugar and lead to insulin spikes and diabetic problems. The Paleo diet should help you minimize or totally avoid sugar, caffeine and refined carbohydrates that wreak havoc on the thyroid.

- *Eat more protein*

Consuming ample protein is beneficial because protein transports the thyroid hormone throughout your body. The best form of protein that Paleo lifestyle advocates for comes from sources such as pastured or organically raised eggs, wild-caught fish, nuts and nut butters. However, you should avoid sources such as energy bars, soy products and GMO foods as they may hinder cell receptors and disrupt the feedback system in your hormonal or endocrine system.

- *Consume healthy fats*

Though too much fat and cholesterol can be dangerous for your body, various hormones require them to enhance normal functioning. An insufficient amount of fat in your diet leads to hormonal imbalances, which affect the functionality of the thyroid hormone.

You can get healthy fats and cholesterol from avocados, fish, coconut milk, flaxseeds and olive oil. Remember that Paleo doesn't permit dairy-based fats such as full fat cottage cheese.

4. Energizes you

The majority of dieters do not know that processed carbs such as sweets or refined grains often spike blood sugar levels and trigger cravings and unnecessary eating.

Worse still, processed foods have low nutritional value and thus cannot be efficiently utilized to generate energy for cells.

However, a Paleo diet that is comprised of fruits and veggies helps supply B-complex vitamins and iron, nutrients that helps with energy, or fuel, in the body. These foods are also rich in fiber and vitamins and offer a more consistent and steady source of energy. Eating such Paleo foods can help generate ample energy in the body that can support metabolic activities without any craving for fast foods.

And, as opposed to similar diet plans that are based on lower caloric intake, this plan doesn't have calorie restrictions. You are allowed to eat healthy foods until you're full, and since you eat whenever you get hungry, there isn't any risk of snacking on processed foods. To improve your energy supply, feed on protein and fiber-rich foods since these facilitate a slow and steady release of calories.

5. Enables you to sleep better

Sleep doesn't come as naturally as you might think for some people. In fact, factors such as diet, stress, disease and other external factors can affect your sleeping patterns. Still, getting 7-9 hours of sleep is vital as it gives the body sufficient time to build and repair muscle and to establish muscle memory from a workout or project. Restful sleep also helps reduce reaction time to stimuli, sharpens your focus and increases energy levels, especially upon waking

The Paleo diet foods are rich in minerals like magnesium and iron as well as vitamins A, B-complex, E and K. These nutrients help calm your nervous system and also create a hormonal response that promotes good sleep. These minerals work on your brain to facilitate faster and restful sleep, and can also help you achieve longer periods of sleeping. To improve your sleep patterns or have a more restful sleep, eat more veggies, fruits and nuts.

6. Controls celiac disease and wheat sensitivity

Gluten is a protein that is found in grains such as barley, wheat, rye and triticale—a cross between rye and wheat. Adopting the Paleo lifestyle means that you ditch wheat (again, you don't eat grains on the Paleo diet) and its related gluten-rich products, foods that may cause allergic reactions in your body. While gluten contributes to weight gain, the sensitivity to gluten due to a condition referred to as *Celiac disease* is the main worry. Based on research, 80 percent of people with celiac diseases in western countries aren't diagnosed yet, and most don't display any gut symptoms. There are also people who suffer other conditions that are indirectly linked to gluten or wheat intolerance, such as non-celiac gluten sensitivity.

Research has shown that removal of gluten from one's diet can help improve undiagnosed celiac disease, whose symptoms include weight gain, fatigue, low bone mineral density, liver failure and various body pains. By removing gluten and other inflammatory substances, the Paleo diet eliminates those allergenic foods that can damage your gut's lining. Cutting out these foods from the diet helps create large midsections, which slows down digestion and allows efficient absorption of nutrients. In addition to that, the Paleo diet plan focuses on more anti-inflammatory foods such as fruits and vegetables, which are rich in antioxidants as well as phytonutrients that help fight related diseases.

7. Promotes healthy brain and cells

The cells in your body are composed of both saturated and unsaturated fats, and these cells depend on a healthy balance between the two fats. The Paleo diet offers a good balance between the fats and therefore facilitates sending of proper messages in and out of the brain. The Paleo diet encourages healthy fats and proteins that are full of omega 3 fatty acids, especially from fish like wild caught salmon. The omega 3 fatty acids are rich in DHA, a substance that promotes a healthy heart, eyes, brain and their proper function. Omega 3 is also known as polyunsaturated fatty acid, and it's vital for normal growth and development.

Furthermore, you also get leaner muscles. This is because the Paleo diet revolves around meat and healthy proteins that should help you feed the muscles and promote a leaner physique. Actually, the ancient man never had excess baggage that comes from accumulated fat, cholesterol or under-developed muscles. When you adopt the diet plan, you achieve a lean and stronger body even if you don't engage in heavy weight training. A leaner body structure should help you handle challenging life situations such as anxiety, depression or economic hardship.

8. Boosts your mood

Lean proteins from fish and poultry, fruits and veggies help balance your energy level, tone your muscles, give you more nutrients and allow you to think more clearly. The vitamin B-complex found in fruits and veggies triggers production of dopamine, a hormone that brings happiness and fights stress. Lean protein foods are rich in omega 3 fatty acids, vitamin E and antioxidants that lower cortisol, or the stress hormone, and thus boost your mood.

To get omega 3 fatty acids, go for cold water fish like tuna and salmon, and nuts like almonds and walnuts to also benefit from antioxidants like vitamin E that fight diseases. Also eat dark-skinned veggies like bell peppers, eggplants, beets, broccoli, spinach and kale, as these have vitamins and other brain-enhancing nutrients. Similarly, eat plenty of fruits like berries, grapes, prunes, cherries and raisins as these have high quality antioxidants that protect your brain cells.

9. Helps control diabetes and high blood sugar

Most people diagnosed with high blood sugar or diabetes are either obese or overweight, so losing weight is often the first step to recovering from the disease. In fact, losing just about 5 to 10 percent of your total weight can help reduce blood sugar levels in your body considerably. The most important step to control blood glucose levels is to eat healthy foods such as proteins and veggies. Carbohydrates have the most effect on your blood sugar levels compared to fats and proteins and that's why the Paleo diet is low in carbs. The diet enables you to avoid processed foods but if you want to take it a bit further to keep your blood sugar levels low, make sure to eat more of the low carb foods like veggies and less of salt and low in saturated and hydrogenated fat vegetable oils. These bad fats are linked to cardiovascular diseases that can easily bring about hypertension, which can make diabetes fatal.

Of course, when you're on the Paleo diet, you eat food that is high in fiber, which promotes satiety and reduces the intake of carbs, while slowing down the conversion of carbs to glucose. Low glycemic foods like fruits and veggies are also recommended as they are low in carbs and can help reverse diabetes symptoms. These low carb, high fiber Paleo foods help control blood sugar levels since they are digested much more slowly, and can prevent your body from releasing excess insulin. They also make you feel full for longer and are a good source of lasting energy.

10. Reduces risk of cancer

Reports show that processed, refined, genetically modified, and artificial foods are linked to cancer and other chronic diseases. You are advised to avoid processed meats such as salami, hot dogs, sausages, ham and nitrate-filled bacon due to chemicals used in their preparation. Ditch any red or processed meat that contains artificial red coloring called heme iron, as research shows it can lead to colon cancer. For example, avoid Microwave popcorn as it contains toxic diacetyl, a chemical that is considered carcinogenic. Even non-organic fruits and veggies are recipes for disaster due to high levels of pesticides and other toxicins. For seafood, farm reared fish may be contaminated with cancer-causing toxins or antibiotics. Furthermore, hydrogenated oils are exposed to chemicals that change their molecular composition and make them carcinogenic.

With the Paleo diet, you avoid all these cancer-causing foods and this ultimately improves your health.

11. Helps you detox

Detox (detoxification) can be explained as the process of removing or neutralizing toxins in the body which otherwise would poison various bodily functions. Detox can benefit you by getting rid of various toxin-related complications such as a bloated stomach, fatigue, poor blood flow and lack of energy.

Detox is very important for your body since accumulation of toxins often leads to inflammation. When you're inflamed, the body lacks the ability to properly carry out the natural detox process, so toxins and waste pile up and this eventually leads to diseases, weight gain and liver problems.

The body is constantly removing waste and toxins through various organs e.g. the kidneys, the liver, the skin and the colon. However, if you eat an excess amount of carbohydrates and processed foods over an extended period, you could easily damage the body's natural detoxification process such that it becomes inefficient. This could even result in gut damage. To fix the problem, you must be deliberate about detoxifying the body by taking measures to actually help the different detox organs to do their job effectively. You can detox using various methods ranging from a fruit and vegetable diet, exercising, and occasional fasting.

Here are the top 3 most effective methods to detoxifying yourself:

- *Sugar detoxification*

This the primary method that works by cutting out all forms of food that have sugars, such as processed foods, alcohol, soda, artificial flavors and other sugar-enriched junk foods.

- *Juice cleanse*

Also referred to as a juice fast, this detox approach involves the consumption of freshly produced juice from veggies and fruits throughout the day. If you adapt the juice fast, you are only allowed to take 4 liters of fresh juice daily, which translates to the caloric load you need. You can also prepare smoothies in order to boost the fiber content in the diet, while not starving the body from the much-needed calories.

- *Clean eating cleanse*

Here you basically eat veggies and fruits, preferably the uncooked or raw. In fact, if you want to practice the juice fast, start with a clean eating cleanse in order to reduce withdrawal symptoms that come from sugar addiction.

12. Helps you overcome sugar addiction

Though it may come as a surprise, research has proven that sugar is to blame for various lifestyle diseases such as obesity, type II diabetes, dementia, cancer, depression and heart disease. In some people, sugar is to blame for impotence and infertility.

Statistics show that an average American takes in around 152 pounds of sugar annually, which translates to 22 teaspoons daily. Our kids consume about 34 teaspoons of sugar, a scenario that explains why many kids are born pre-diabetic or diabetic. It's hard to cut down on sugar especially because of its availability in most foods, its sweetness and its long-term addiction.

Science suggests that the reason that sugar causes addiction is because of its effect on the brain. When you consume sugar, it stimulates production of chemicals called opioids that produce euphoria, and dopamine. The brain chemical dopamine actually monitors the brain's reward and pleasure centers. Once sugar gets to the brain, the body's pain sensors are temporally switched off, and instead, the brain receives a 'sweet message' signal. Once your brain experiences the pleasure, you'll always reach for sugar for similar feelings. Similar to other addictive substances, the higher the amount of sugar that you consume, the more cravings you get. Sugar can also dull your taste buds over time and thus you'll need a higher amount to achieve the same sugary hit.

Another problem with sugar is that it can influence your behavior. Research has shown that people predisposed to other addictions could be more addicted to sugar and hence crave more of it. These people get addicted to junk food and lose control over their regulation, as their brain chemistry is altered by hormonal changes. Addiction to sugar works on a similar level as addiction to cannabis, nicotine or amphetamines. In fact, addicts trying to recover from gaming, alcohol or drug addiction, report that they struggle to ditch their sugar addiction too. By banning most processed and high sugar ingredients, the Paleo diet helps you fight your sugar addiction. Once you ditch the sugary or junk foods, you can then focus on healthier micronutrients and phytochemicals to help you combat the altered brain chemistry and break this cycle.

In order to achieve these benefits, you need to strictly follow the Paleo diet by only buying foods that are approved by the diet. You need to avoid refined carbs, foods with added sugars, saturated fats and other junk foods that cause obesity and diseases. With all the above benefits in mind, let's now discuss how you can get started on the diet as a complete beginner to ensure that you start without any major challenges.

Getting Started on the Paleo Diet

The easiest way to fully succeed in the Paleo diet is to start making small positive changes against unhealthy eating. In other words, cut off one unhealthy ingredient at a time. But why is that important? Well, when lowering the amount of processed foods in your diet, taking off one thing at a time is more effective than removing everything on the menu that is non-Paleo. This way, you can help your brain adjust and incorporate these and the corresponding changes slowly. Let's take it a bit further:

1. Decide on the source of your food

As you switch to Paleo, ensure that you get your ingredients from credible sources free from chemicals used in conventional crops and animals.

First, avoid eating food grown with artificial pesticides, fertilizers and other additives, along with meat from animals fed with GMOs or those that are processed. Thus, it might be advisable to buy organic produce or animal meat straight from the farms where you can see exactly how they have been raised.

2. Stock up your kitchen

It takes time and effort to transform your pantry to what a Paleo lifestyle calls for. While it's time consuming, having a variety of foods is important when transiting into an absolute Paleo diet as this ensures you get a variety of tastes. The initial step to a happy transition is to buy a small supply of fresh whole foods, fruits and veggies; and then gradually increase the collection of these foods. It's advisable to buy food that can last long in your kitchen such as oils and butters, nuts, seeds and spices.

Here's a simple guide of what you may consider:

—Get lots of Omega 3 rich nuts, among them macadamia, pecans, hazel nuts, walnuts, pine nuts, cashew nuts and almonds. Nuts and seeds are good snack options as they require little or no preparation and are satiating.

—Stock up on natural spices such as black pepper, cayenne powder, turmeric powder, onion powder, garlic powder, coriander powder, nutmeg powder, cumin powder and cinnamon, among others. Check the list of ingredients to detect any artificial filler.

—Stock up on healthy oils and butters such as cold-pressed olive oil, flaxseed oil, virgin coconut oil, nut butter and organic cacao butter. Avoid hydrogenated oils and trans fats that come with most baked products.

- If it is necessary to sweeten food, only buy organic sweeteners such as raw honey, organic coconut palm nectar, stevia and natural flavor enhancers such as tamari and sea salt.

3. Begin to plan your meals

As a beginner in the Paleo diet, developing a regular meal plan can help you to rapidly adapt to the diet and thus reduce craving for sugary foods. When planning your diet, you can choose to begin with 3 meals per day (every 5-6 hours). This should help you stay satiated without causing any metabolic breakdown.

Maintaining a favorable diet plan or timing for meals can facilitate absorption, fight cravings and make you stick to the diet. To quicken weight loss, try to eat breakfast within the first hour of waking, preferably as the largest meal of the day. You can eat about 30-40 grams of protein, non-starchy veggies such as broccoli along with a fruit to start your day.

4. Start small with recipes

The Paleo lifestyle demands that you make substitutes for processed foods and also introduce other food options you may not be accustomed to. If you find your new meal plan hard to implement, begin with those simple meals that require locally available ingredients from supermarkets, grocers or local farmer's markets. Get a variety of foods by making a list of nuts and seeds, herbs or other ingredients to form part of your diet. For instance, start with fresh fruits for breakfast, or a fresh fruit smoothie without dairy. For dairy substitutes, choose simple recipes that incorporate almond milk or coconut cream milk.

5. Incorporate more veggies

Veggies have ample vitamins, such as vitamin A, which boost your immunity and vision, and vitamin K, which promotes healthy bones. Since vegetables are lower in calories and carbs, they are recommended for weight loss and to address lifestyle diseases like diabetes. You also benefit from heart-healthy fiber while promoting satiety and curbing overeating.

To start eating veggies, choose those unprocessed organic varieties that come straight from the farm, and consume 2 ½-3 cups daily. To ensure you achieve satiety, eat hummus or carrot sticks as snacks, begin meals with a salad, or add onions and peppers to an egg omelet.

6. Add a few fresh fruits

Fruits are sweet and nutritious, rich in potassium and rich in vitamin A. You need potassium to control blood pressure and vitamin A helps promote a healthier immune system. When choosing fruits, go for the unprocessed variety, though canned, frozen or dried fruits can also be healthy for you. The recommended fruit intake is about 1 ½ - 2 cups daily and this should help you get fiber and lose weight provided that you don't drink fruit juices.

7. Double your protein intake

Protein rich foods are the core part of your Paleo diet. Healthy proteins come from pastured eggs, fish, and seafood such as shrimp, salmon, haddock, and trout. Foods such as wild-caught salmon provide the best sources of fats and proteins that you can get. The fish is rich in omega 3 fatty acids, which contain DHA, a mineral that promotes healthy functioning of the heart and the brain. You can get omega 3 fatty acids from eggs and grass-fed meats from chicken, turkey, goat, lamb and pig, among others.

When you have researched and come up with a proper diet and plan to get you started, it is important to maintain a few things in order to make your goal a success. Many dieters are disappointed when they structure a well-laid plan but do not get the desired results. If you follow the following tips, you are bound to get very good results from your diet.

How to Make Your Paleo Diet a Success

1. Practice meal timing

Nutritional experts recommend that we consume at least 3 meals a day in a bid to help monitor blood sugar levels, and to keep hunger and cravings at bay. However, be aware that during the Stone Age, our ancestors had no particular eating pattern or timing for meals, and their meal times depended on the availability of food.

However, as a beginner in the Paleo diet, eating regularly can help you rapidly adapt to the diet and thus reduce your craving for sugary foods. However, after the body becomes accustomed to Paleo, try to have 3 meals per day, say after every 5 hours.

Research has shown that consumption of 3 meals daily with a 5-hour gap between them can help you stay satiated without causing metabolic breakdown. You shouldn't wait longer than 5 hours since the liver and pancreas would stay on an "alert" mode, whereas too soon can overwork these organs. Maintaining a favorable timing for meals facilitates absorption, fights cravings, and prevents possible health complications. To quicken weight loss, try to eat breakfast within the first hour of waking, preferably as the largest meal of the day.

In the morning, the body has already starved throughout the night, which essentially means you need sufficient nutrients to rebuild it. Breakfast is also important in helping you realize the natural feelings of both hunger and fullness. It enables you to stop worrying about hunger since the next meal or snack is in your plan. Eating a healthy breakfast should help trigger the metabolism to start burning calories throughout the day. In fact, if you don't have a healthy breakfast, you could affect your weight loss goals negatively because of cravings and overeating.

For an energy-packed breakfast, strive to eat about 30-40 grams of protein, non-starchy veggies such as broccoli, and a fruit.

2. Control how you handle your hunger

If you're already addicted to eating food or are obsessed with eating certain foods, it is probable that you often fantasize about it. This leads to binging or emotional eating where you eat abnormal amounts of food and you're totally unable to control or stop the cravings. In most cases, emotional eating lasts for about 2 hours, though a number of people may eat all day!

The bad thing is that you eat even when not feeling hungry and progress to eat more after being full. After binge-eating, you often feel guilty and depressed.

The Paleo diet can help you overcome emotional eating through these recommended approaches:

- ***Give up the addictive foods***

Though you can't choose to be addicted, it's possible to give up those foods that cause addiction for the sake of recovery. A number of addictive people have managed to fight the addiction by abstaining from the addictive substance as opposed to negotiating with it. To regain your freedom, you have to give up the 'feel-good' sugary foods and thus embark on the journey towards the recovery.

The hardest part of this remedy is that you must be willing to undergo a period of temptations and discomfort. You should actually be aware that withdrawal symptoms are evident during your initial stages of abstinence, and that urges might return. Relapse is mostly triggered by the desire to escape the emotional distress caused by forgoing what you like most. Try to manage stress and identify those factors that trigger stress to succeed in the recovery process. Nonetheless, the best comfort is that the longer you abstain from those cravings, the easier it will be to keep avoiding them.

- ***Always have something to eat***

Make sure to eat at least a couple hundred calories every five to six hours even when not necessarily feeling hungry. This makes it a lot easier to control your emotions, and avoid emotional eating.

Keeping Paleo foods in your fridge may be a good idea especially if you are an emotional eater. You will eventually have to find other ways to deal with your emotions rather than jumping on every cupcake or chocolate that you find. This helps change your eating perspective by changing what you eat, regardless of whether you are actually hungry or not.

- *Do not skip meals*

Eating at least 3 meals a day and sticking to set meal patterns will go a long way towards restoring normal eating patterns. Skipping meals will often lead to a binge, so your eating should be scheduled appropriately.

You should also stop dieting and starving and instead focus on nutritious food making up most of your food—banning specific types of food may make you crave for them in the long run when you're just starting out.

Another problem associated with skipping meals is that it can affect your blood sugar level and prohibit effective weight loss. You don't want to add more health problems before solving the primary issue of uncontrollable eating!

- ***Eat fat-releasing foods***

In case you feel like indulging, try fat-releasing foods instead, as they can help you feel fuller and thus avoid craving high calorie foods. For example, a tablespoon of honey has up to 64 fat releasing calories, while a hard-boiled egg has up to 70 calories and is rich in protein that has fat releasing properties. With dark chocolate, you'll get 168 calories in a 1 ounce square but it also has a fat-releaser.

This book consistently advises you to cut all dairy intakes. But for those who still consume yogurt: Eating yogurt thrice a day and simultaneously cutting down calorie intake by 500 allows you lose more weight. This is because the calcium from low-fat yogurt triggers a hormonal response that hinders synthesis of fat. The process helps improve fat breakdown and eventual weight loss.

- ***Keep a food diary***

Keeping a food diary is the best method of tracking your eating patterns. You will be able to see the ingredients that help suppress your cravings.

Trying various Paleo-friendly foods can also help solve your emotional eating tendencies and thus improve your mood and related problems, and keeping track of them in a diary can help you see the pattern.

3. Eat Paleo-friendly carbs

Paleo is a low carb diet but you can still enjoy substantial amounts of carbohydrates from fresh vegetables and fruits. The calories you get from these carbs is way less than from eating processed foods or grains.

Furthermore, if the good calories are higher than the restricted ones, chances are high that your diet will be a success. Remember that the calories to completely avoid include those from milk products, nuts, artificial sweeteners, grains and processed meats.

However, if you find yourself unsuccessful even after selecting the right calories and avoiding the restricted ones, you may want to just forget about them all. Start fresh without the veggies and fruits and see if you lose weight this time.

4. Ditch "low carb" factory-packed products

The majority of processed foods are rich in fat, added sugars, excess sodium and other artificial flavors, which can add empty calories to your diet and lead to weight gain. What you may not know is that most of the labels that show the carb count usually have hidden values that are allowed by law to be rounded off. Eating too much of these causes an imbalance of the total calorie count in your diet.

So when buying food, the check list of ingredients and ditch those packaged goodies with ingredients that you can't understand. As single ingredients, packaged foods like baby spinach and canned tuna are both healthy and rich in fiber and vitamins. One way of eating healthy is to prepare your own homemade food such as granola bars and tomato sauce, macaroni and cheese. Doing so will help you prepare pure and whole nutritious food instead of going for the readymade products.

5. Eat healthier fats

You should ensure that most of the fats in your diet are good fats. The good fats come mostly from unprocessed meats and olive and nut oils in that they promote heart health, weight loss, good mood and increased energy. Fats from processed foods are considered bad. Try to swap unhealthy saturated fat sources like cheese and butter with alternatives like canola oil, coconut or olive oil and those oils found in fish or nuts.

Unsaturated fatty acids promote heart health by boosting the good HDL cholesterol; and most of them are liquid at room temperature.

The best fats come from olive oil, rapeseed, hazelnuts and almonds, with avocado and pumpkin seed also containing around 15 percent of fat. These fats are useful in lowering the level of low-density lipoprotein and can inhibit the occurrence of heart disease. Let's see these foods along with the amount of monounsaturated fat in them:

- Sesame seeds -20 per cent

- Avocados -12 per cent

- Pumpkin seeds -16 per cent

- Cashews -28 per cent

- Brazil nuts -26 per cent

- Almonds -35 per cent

- Hazelnuts -50 per cent

- Rapeseed oil -60 per cent

- Olive oil -73 per cent

To avoid solid fats, try topping your salads with nuts in place of cream cheese or avocado in place of mayonnaise or peanut butter.

6. Don't sweeten your foods

Added sugars cause insulin insensitivity, binge eating and weight gain along with lifestyle diseases like diabetes among others. Eating a healthy diet requires cutting down on added sugars by eating less baked goods, candies or sodas. In addition, choose unsweetened varieties of healthy foods like yogurt and tomato sauce.

Simply go for foods that have no sugar, or use healthier alternatives like organic honey and stevia.

The American Heart Association recommends a maximum of 6 teaspoons of sugar for women and 9 teaspoons for men per day. Try to go even lower than that!

7. Limit salt intake

Excess salt beyond the recommended 2,300 mg per day can raise your blood pressure. That's not all; salt has an impact on your kidneys and can make your body retain water. This excess water increases your blood pressure and this strains your heart, arteries and brain leading to high pressure in blood flow. To reduce salt intake, try the following tips and tricks:

—Cut down on processed foods, since the majority of packaged goodies have excess sodium.

—Consider replacing common salt with things like vinegar, citrus and various herbs.

—Buy ingredients or foods that do not contain any salt

—If eating out, don't order veggies that are topped with sauces. Instead, order only steamed veggies

—For fish, only order steamed or boiled versions and instead season using natural herbs and spices. Avoid spices with added ingredients, salts or preservatives.

—Do not use condiments that are high in sodium such as mustard, ketchup, and pickles.

8. Moderate gluten intake

Gluten refers to proteins found in wheat's endosperm, which constitutes 80% of all proteins found in wheat. While gluten isn't properly digested into amino acids like other proteins, it also contains the *gliadin* protein that is linked to <u>uncontrollable appetite</u> and is a recipe for weight gain. But exactly how is eating wheat associated with gaining a few pounds? Well, much of the wheat-containing food that you eat tends to have a high glycemic load that increases your blood sugar level. An increase in blood glucose levels triggers release of the insulin hormone to help uptake or absorb glucose into body cells. A higher level of insulin hormone means that glucose is absorbed into the body's cells at higher rate, which makes you feel hungry a few hours after eating.

The hunger or cravings that you develop after eating wheat products makes you consume higher glycemic foods. In fact, foods that you could be intolerant to or would like to regulate like buttered toast or wheat thins are the ones that you crave most. In simple terms this could be described as "addiction to gluten" which occurs for one main reason: Wheat has a protein called gliadin that breaks down into peptides that can cross into the brain and bind your morphine receptors. Once this happens, the body reacts to intolerant foods by creating addictive narcotics called opioid endorphins. This effect creates a euphoria-like reaction to the bread, which is blamed for increased appetite and food addiction, which with time makes you gain weight.

Another problem with wheat is that gluten also affects the leptin hormone, which controls your brain and tells it when you are full. Once this happens, you become leptin resistant, and as a result, your brain no longer sends messages to control the amount of food that you are eating. This will lead you to consume extra food particularly carbohydrate-high food with a substantial amount of gluten, thus leading, to weight increase.

So what can you do about this entire problem? Well, these tips can help you reduce the amount of gluten in your diet:

1. Read food labels when you shop

Packaged foods do have allergen labeling that includes lists of allergens and gluten used to make the product, regardless of how little was used. Look for any mention of wheat, spelt, oats, rye or Kamut, as well as any other grain that may have been breaded with gluten. In a majority of products such ingredients could be highlighted in bold. Try companies that sell gluten-free foods or instead order from Amazon, especially if you want to buy in bulk.

2. Ask for details at grocery stores and restaurants.

Even for naturally gluten-free foods, there's a possibility of cross contamination. Get details on how food served in restaurants is prepared and the type of equipment used. Gluten-free foods are best made using separate utensils or pots and pans that are thoroughly washed.

3. Choose animal protein carefully

Be aware that marinated chicken or fish contain gluten just like bread batter that covers meat or fish. If you cannot tolerate these foods, consider eliminating them from your diet totally.

4. Eat plenty of protein-rich meat to replace iron-rich breads and cereals. Some common meats that you can eat are fish, but make sure that they are not covered

with bread-batter, and this may lead to some changes in your weight.

5. Chicken stock and most canned soups contain a relatively high amount of gluten because they are thickened with processed wheat flour. The majority of pasta sauces, condiments, stocks and gravies contain wheat flour, and that's why you should read labels to ensure you do not accidentally buy gluten rich foods. If in doubt, you can make your own pasta sauces or gravies using alternatives like potato starch, and arrowroot starch and corn flour to thicken them. Also prepare your soup from scratch or choose gluten free varieties.

9. Swap juices for green smoothies

Unlike fruit juices that are loaded with sugar, green smoothies are high in antioxidants, which detoxify the body from liver-poisoning toxins. Furthermore, green smoothies are also easy to digest while providing important nutrients for your body. Smoothies made from fruits and veggies are also rich in dietary fiber, which helps in slowing down the uptake of sugar. As opposed to other foods, fiber gently passes out undigested through your digestive system, which in turn facilitates slow digestion and eventually boosts satiety.

Another great thing about green smoothies is that over time, you start craving more of the green smoothies as opposed to unhealthy snacks like potato chips. Once you get there, you are sure to achieve objectives such as detox and weight loss. For better results, try preparing homemade smoothies as these can help you have control of your eating and prevent sugar spikes or cravings.

10. Substitute non-Paleo foods

Adopting a Paleo diet doesn't mean that you should completely do away with your favorite foods, carbs or sweets. The key point is learning how to substitute that unhealthy diet with healthy alternatives. In this case, Paleo diet isn't too restrictive; you can get your bread or meat through a few workarounds. Replace those starchy foods with flour alternatives like nut and coconut floor. This list features those foods you can easily substitute for the same delicious taste.

- *All-purpose flour substitutes*

You don't have to struggle with forsaking your delicious wheat products because you can effectively use other non-grain flours such as coconut flour. The reason coconut flour is recommended is that it has low carb content, is high in fiber and is also rich in proteins.

About 2 tablespoons of coconut flour has 5 g of proteins, 4g of fat and 11g of fiber. Coconut flour has healthy fats, as it's a medium-chain saturated fat that can shield you from heart disease.

Note: Coconut flour can absorb more water than wheat flour especially because of its high fiber content.

You can also use almond flour or other nut flours for wheat flour substitution. Almond flour is rich in zinc, iron, selenium, calcium, magnesium, proteins and vitamins E and B. Nut-based flours do not contain gluten; thus, you need to add eggs to act as a binder, or use arrowroot flour for a crumby texture. Buy almond, blanch and grind in a food processor to make homemade flour. Apart from almond and coconut flour, also look for tapioca flour and other non-grain flours.

- *Dairy or milk substitutes*

Instead of cow's milk that contains allergens such as lactose, use almond or coconut milk in recipes that require a creamy or milk flavor. Almond milk is suitable for blending other ingredients and actually has real milk flavor when used in a recipe. In addition, coconut milk, as well as with coconut cream, works as a milk alternative despite the strong flavor.

Choose coconut milk that isn't coated with synthetic ingredients such as bisphenol-A, and one without added flavors, preservatives or sugars.

Coconut cream is a good substitute for regular cream. It has a great taste, and doesn't have allergens or those fats and added ingredients in processed creams.

- ***Cooking oils substitutes***

Instead of margarine, use ghee, which is a Paleo friendly butter with many impurities removed and with an amazing flavor. Also, try coconut oil in place of vegetable oils such as sunflower or corn oil, which are processed.

Olive oil also replaces canola oil perfectly in making salad dressings or mayonnaise, though you need the purest form with no added ingredients. In place of peanut butter, use almond butter that comes in crunchy and smooth forms and doesn't come from legumes. Remember to avoid hydrogenated or partially hydrogenated oils, and those high in oleic compounds.

- ***Starchy carb substitutes***

For those into potatoes, mashed potatoes, potatoes chips and French fries, try sweet potatoes, as these can replace all recipes involving regular potatoes. It's even easier to adopt sweet potatoes for hash browns for breakfast.

Also, try mashed cauliflower as it looks like potatoes and is tasty. Alternatively, you can use kale chips, which offer a similar crunch to potato chips, together with proteins, fiber, minerals and vitamins. Kale chips are easy to prepare as you only need organic seasonings, suitable plant-based oils and kale leaves.

For bread, go for Paleo alternatives that contain Paleo ingredients like coconut, zucchini, banana or pumpkin. You can use any flower substitute, like coconut or almond flour, for your breads.

For your favorite pasta dish, use zucchini instead, or make lasagna by subbing in zucchini strips to make a healthy meal. Zucchini is also a substitute for spaghetti dishes, such as squash; and allows you eat more veggies. Cauliflower rice is a suitable replacement for regular rice, where you just chop cauliflower to resemble rice. Use this rice as the main or side dish in any of your recipes.

- ***Substitutes for sugars***

You need to avoid sugars and preservatives by using alternatives such as maple syrup and raw honey as well as stevia powder. When it comes to sweet goodies such as milk chocolate that has added sugars and milk, go for dark chocolate instead. Dark chocolate is rich in antioxidants and has a great taste. Alternatively, you can use cocoa powder for the same Paleo experience.

- *Use flax meal for bread crumbs*

Flax meal is useful for holding those meatballs together and for coating the chicken parmesan the same way bread crumbs do, while still giving you that same flavor you like. On top of this, you get additional omega 3 fatty acids from flaxseeds. You can also go for chia seeds, which are also rich in omega 3.

11. Get enough nutrients

As part of your Paleo lifestyle agenda, you need to get sufficient amounts of vitamins and minerals, which support various metabolic functions. Why is this important? Well, this is important because they stimulate weight loss by strengthening your body cells and muscles, bones and supplying the required energy. Vitamins such as B help your cells make protein, release energy and manufacture serotonin; a brain chemical. This vitamin comes from salmon, sardines, lean meat, and eggs.

Apart from vitamins, minerals like omega 3 and magnesium can directly boost your mood and combat disorders such as stress, depression and anxiety. Diets that contain Omega-3 essential fatty acids, such as cold-water fish and salmon, provide the body with DHA and EPA. Other minerals like magnesium play many roles, with the most important function being production of DNA or RNA, and moderation of your heartbeat. To boost magnesium intake, eat bananas, roasted nuts, and steamed spinach.

12. Exercise regularly

The Paleolithic man did not become lean by only eating meats, fruits, seeds, nuts and vegetables; he spent his days running away from predators, hunting, foraging etc. You too ought to be physically active if you have any hopes of losing weight and becoming lean like the Paleolithic man. You could be on a busy schedule but nonetheless commit at least one hour of your day, four days a week to exercise.

There are two types of training to consider: strength training and aerobics. Study them and decide on how to approach them. If you are going to do only one, then begin with the strength training since it is the most important when losing weight. The other form of training facilitates alternate periods of intense activity with bursts of slower recovery. Try 20-30 minutes of bike riding, walking or swimming to rev your metabolism and thus burn more calories. With interval training, you can develop leaner muscles to further rev the metabolism and to assist you in breaking that weight loss plateau.

13. Know how to eat out

Sometimes, especially if working outside the home, you have to eat out. It's also normal to travel or get invited into a friend's party where organic and unprocessed food may not be available. How do you ensure you keep your intake of processed foods low in these situations? Here are some ideas:

- ***Carry food with you***

If going out for work or an event, it's good to carry a lunch bag that comprises of leftovers and snack foods. Snacks like hummus, seeds, nuts and protein bars can help you ditch processed and sweet foods sold at your local restaurant.

If you must go to a restaurant, call ahead to ask if you are allowed to bring your own salad dressing and order a salad.

If you're invited to a friend's house, you can consider bringing some Paleo friendly foods with you to avoid being tempted to eat what you shouldn't be eating. When you travel, have ideas in your mind for places to eat or instead reach for gluten-free snacks like almonds, asparagus and chopped veggies. Ensure that you always ask about the food available to make sure you don't unknowingly eat processed food.

- **Plan for substitutes/Snacks**

Ensure that you plan for your entire day or week's supply of food to avoid resorting to sugary and unhealthy foods. Dehydrated fruit slices and flaxseeds crackers make a good choice. Just make it your custom to plan in advance and include various raw snack recipes into your kitchen schedule.

14. Eat raw food

Raw food can be described as that which hasn't been cooked, microwaved, processed, genetically modified, irradiated or exposed to herbicides or pesticides. The practice of eating raw food is aimed that conserving the enzymes that help in both absorption and digestion of food. It is believed that cooking kills or denatures enzymes found in food and thus forces the body to work harder to reproduce such enzymes. Deficiency of important enzymes in the body is blamed for weight gain, accelerated aging, deficiency of nutrients and digestive breakdown. Worse still, cooking destroys the nutritional value of some foods, specifically the vegetables. For instance, the cancer fighting sulforaphanes found in broccoli are denatured after cooking, and most of the vitamin C and folate found in other veggies is also destroyed by cooking.

In a Paleo raw food diet, you consume a high amount of fruits and veggies, sprouts, nuts and seeds and raw almond butter. For fats, you aim for raw coconut butter, raw virgin coconut oil and extra virgin cold processed olive oil. You can have herbal teas and freshly squeezed vegetable juice now and then. Recommendations about raw food types that you can eat include:

1. Fresh fruits and vegetables—store a wide variety of root veggies, greens and herbs in the fridge. Always ensure that your fresh fruits such as berries and veggies like fresh lettuce or seaweed are organic.

2. Sprouts, nuts and seeds

Always keep about 2 mason jars of sprouted nuts and seeds in the fridge and some sprouted sunflower as well. Also keep almonds, soaked for preservation, in the fridge to use, but you should change the water daily for a storage period of 5 days. Nut and seed butters are also welcome in your raw food diet.

To help easily germinate or sprout the ingredients, soak the food in water for a period of time, at least 2 hours. For better results, soak your food overnight.

Start your dieting with dried, raw and organic nuts as well as seeds.

-First rinse your seeds or nuts and then put them into a glass container.

-Add water at room temperature to cover and soak your raw food, preferably overnight.

-Once done, rinse them a number of times and then use.

3. You can also have dried fruits

Obtain a variety of them such as dried apples, mangoes, apricots, coconut, pineapple, goji berries, cranberries, raisins and dates. Dates serve as preferable sweeteners, especially for raw food desserts.

4. Spices, fresh and dried herbs

You should incorporate them to help flavor your raw meals. You can add natural sweeteners such as raw honey and stevia. You can also use organic and unfiltered apple cider vinegar, which is rich in malic acid, and can aid in the digestion of proteins.

5. Oils such as refrigerated hemp oil, cold-pressed olive oil and refrigerated flax seed oil.

I truly believe that you now know enough about starting out on the Paleo diet as well as how to set yourself up for success from the onset. However, even with the best of intentions, you could make some mistakes along the way. Let's discuss some of these and how to avoid them to increase your odds of success.

Mistakes to Avoid When on the Paleo Diet

No doubt, you want quick and positive results after being on the Paleo diet for some time. And since you have the necessary advice to set you off on the Paleo diet, let's see some of the common mistakes dieters make when on this diet:

1: Eating too many carbs

It has not yet been proven what a low carb diet should contain, but most people say that it should be between 100-150 grams of carbohydrates per day. This very effective strategy has worked for many dieters when sticking to real and proper unprocessed foods.

Nonetheless, depending on your basal metabolic rate, this amount of carbs can be too much when you want to fully breakdown fats into energy. Thus, to be on the safe side (especially with regards to pushing your body to a point of using more of the stored body fat), you are advised to keep your carb consumption to below 50 grams per day by consuming dark leafy-green veggies.

However, remember that carbs don't only come from grains and processed foods but also from fruits and veggies. You need to check the carb content for fresh veggies before eating them. Don't be scared of eating salads often; however, choose low-carb fruits and veggies. Since fruits could be rich in carbs, try selecting fruits such as berries; and avoid all grains, as already stated, whether whole or processed.

2: Excessive protein intake

Protein forms a very big part of the Paleo diet. In fact, protein is a very important nutrient in the body since it improves satiety and influences the process of burning fats. For that reason, many dieters believe that eating more protein therefore means more fat is burned in your body, leading to weight loss.

On the contrary, eating too much protein, especially for those who get most of their protein from animals, causes some of the amino acids in the protein to be converted to glucose in a process referred to as *gluconeogenesis*. If the converted glucose is produced in excess, most of it is stored and thus prevents the body from breaking down fats. In order to be safe, it is advisable to have a ratio of low carbs, high fats and moderate proteins.

In general, an intake higher than 250 grams of proteins daily can hinder the body from excreting the toxic byproducts of protein metabolism such as ammonia. Furthermore, once the proteins aren't fully processed and get into the intestines, the undigested protein undergoes fermentation through the gut bacteria and yields inflammatory products. In extreme cases, a protein-only diet can cause loss of calcium and damage your kidneys.

So exactly how much protein do you require? Well, if you work out, 1.5-2.0 grams per kg of body weight can match well with a low-carb diet. And if you don't work out as much, try to maintain protein intake to below 1.5 g/kg and ensure that the protein comes from organic, grass fed/wild animals and seafood like fatty wild-caught salmon or kelp.

3: Fear of eating fat

Most of the calories we eat on the typical American diet come from carbohydrates such as sugars and grains. But when on the Paleo diet, you may decide to remove most of the sources of carbohydrates without a proper replacement.

You may believe that having a diet with no carbs and no fats is the best formula to achieving success. This approach is very wrong in that you're starving your body of essential nutrients and vitamins.

As you should now know, fats and starch are the main sources of energy for the body so if you completely ditch starch, you need Paleo-friendly substitutes to give you the energy your body needs. There are healthy fats that you can go for which include the saturated, monounsaturated and the omega3s. While you may choose to adjust your diet, the total caloric intake from fats should constitute around 55-75% of your diet.

4: Low intake of indigestible fiber

It's a fact that eating more animal protein and less plant-based proteins may make you eat less fiber. So why should you eat fiber and where does it come from? Dietary fiber helps slow down glucose absorption into the blood, which means it doesn't allow a rapid rise in your blood sugar level as simple carbs do. Fiber also assists in the production and storing of fats in the body, besides making you feel fuller for longer and fighting cravings.

While fiber is hardly present in meat, you can get it from a few Paleo-friendly ingredients such as fruits and veggies. You can obtain soluble fiber from foods such as grapes, kiwi, pomegranates, blackberries, raspberries, tart cherries and blueberries. Low glycemic and fiber-rich veggies that are your best choice include artichokes, asparagus, summer squash and broccoli.

Even after trying all of the above, you might still experience some challenges while following the Paleo diet. The question you might be having is; why is that so? Let me answer that question next:

Why the Paleo Diet is Not Working for You

If you are on this diet and are not satisfied by the results, then there are some things that you are not doing right. Here are a few of them:

1. You are not eating real food

It's not just enough to concentrate on the Paleo diet. Try replacing the carbohydrates you ditched with proper nutritious foods such as fish, vegetables, eggs, meats and maybe healthy fats to lose weight.

Keep away from treats such as brownies and the like and only eat them as occasional snacks.

In addition, you may not be cutting down on carbohydrates as much as you should.

Everyone has a different level of sensitivity to carbs compared. In your case, you may want to reduce the amount of carbohydrates even further. It may come down to stopping fruits altogether, although berries are still recommended.

2. You're cheating too much

If you're struggling with weight, there could be some truth that you have an eating addiction. More often than not, people with eating addictions cannot help themselves when they are near unhealthy foods. Yes, you have the ability to control yourself when eating healthy foods but according to you, taking cheat meals occasionally isn't bad. You have to gradually find ways of completely ditching the non-Paleo and processed foods.

Even if you are susceptible to a food addiction, try to avoid cheat meals since they are more harmful than helpful. But what's the way out? Is there any alternative to having too many cheat days?

Well, you can adopt various creative ways to snack and enjoy what you eat without going overboard, if only you have healthy snacks with you. For instance, protein-rich nuts, roasted pumpkin seeds or hard-boiled eggs can come in handy.

Moreover, leftovers can help simplify your life, especially if served as a lunch or snack.

Lastly, store your meat and veggies separately after cooking, and only combine a small amount when serving. This helps you have stored food, which can be combined with sauces to make a complete meal. Alternatively, eat salads for lunch, by piling them with suitable veggies and then topping with protein.

Your target should be to eat at least 2 low-carb snacks per day especially after breakfast, after lunch and dinner, to help remain full. For additional snack options, try using nuts, tuna, smoked salmon, hard boiled eggs, leftover diced pork chops, leftover pulled chicken or taco meat. Also try out frying veggies such as peppers and onions in lard or coconut oil until crisp, and then throwing in some herbs and spices, like garlic and black pepper. And if away from home, try Asian snacks such as dried anchovies and kelp chips prepared in coconut or palm oil.

3. You lack sufficient sleep

Sleep is very important if you are struggling to lose weight. Lack of sleep can make you feel really hungry which ultimately leads you to emotionally eating. It also hinders you from effective exercise because you wake up feeling tired and lazy in the morning.

However, be aware that doing everything by the book doesn't necessarily mean that you will get desired results as far as sleeping is concerned. For instance, if you have a sleeping disorder, make an appointment with your doctor, as most sleeping disorders are treatable.

4. You are stressed

Know that if you are in a stressful environment, it could cause an imbalance of your hormone levels and an increase in the levels of hormones such as cortisol.

This state of fight or flight causes you to experience increased cravings for unhealthy foods and to have an increased appetite. Try to reduce stress by doing breathing exercises and reading various motivational books.

Also closely related to this problem, you could be fighting a medical condition or taking prescription medication. Some drugs, such as anti-depressants have weight gain as a side effect. So if going through a certain medical treatment, visit your doctor to find out if there are any substitute drugs available that you can take. While many dieters overlook this point, doing this and everything else right will help you lose weight in the long run.

5. You are not staying hydrated

To some extent, carbs attract water and enable the body to remain hydrated, and thus a low-carb diet such as Paleo can cause dehydration and strain the kidneys.

Water also helps flush out toxins from the kidney and facilitates weight loss, as the body usually binds toxins that are within the body using fat cells to keep them away from vital organs.

Unfortunately, many dieters on low-carb diets are afraid of water retention and thus regulate water intake in a bid to see immediate results on the scale. Though good weight loss can encourage you to stick to a low-carb diet, the body quickly adjusts and instead adopts other ways of water retention.

Did you know that dehydration also triggers cravings? It can also interrupt the beta-oxidation process that deals with metabolism of fats as energy sources. If you drink coffee daily, ensure you also consume a 6-8 glasses of water as well.

6. You don't eat regularly!

The majority of dieters want to only eat when hungry and to make matters worse they consume one or two large meals in a day. It may come as a surprise to you, but obesity specialists advise that eating regular and spaced meals can help minimize cravings and hunger, as this keeps the body in an anabolic or active state.

Doing so also helps you avoid unhealthy snacking, as you never have to get hungry, feel deprived or feel any urge to cheat.

Ensure that you eat every 2-3 hours, and choose complex carbs and lean proteins at every meal, or an alternative protein drink with some fruit. Proteins boost satiety and when combined with complex carbs help stabilize blood sugar.

To get a refreshing change, consider incorporating various veggies and seasonings while you research recipes. Also substitute saturated or trans fats with unsaturated and omega 3 fatty acids as these help lower risk of heart disease.

7. You don't eat fermented foods

Yes, Paleo is all about fresh foods but you could be missing something very important for your weight loss and health in general. Fermented foods should be on your to-buy list so you can use them to top your fresh produce.

This is because these foods work as digestive enzymes due to the presence of probiotics or good bacteria. Gut bacteria, commonly referred to as gut flora, help restore your immunity and facilitate effective digestion and absorption of foods. Better still, fermented foods have nutrients that help nourish the body.

If new to fermented foods, begin with little amounts daily and slowly increase. Try fermented foods such as kombucha, tempeh, kefir, kimchi or fermented pickles. Both cabbage juice and sauerkraut are also strong stimulants for your body and help boost the production of stomach acid. Try to add a few teaspoons of fermented sauerkraut or cabbage juice to water or food to improve digestion.

8. You are exposed to chemicals

The truth is that in today's world, toxic substances exist everywhere i.e. in the water we drink and the air we breathe. However, this does not mean that you should give up on your quest to keeping your intake of toxins low.

But how do you do that? Let's get to the basics. Most conventionally grown crops are sprayed with chemicals such as herbicides, pesticides and chemical fertilizers mainly to better the yield. However, such chemicals are harmful for your body and environment, as they play a part in depleting soils and contaminating seas and rivers.

As you switch to the Paleo lifestyle, ensure that you get organically grown crops and pastured animal products right from the source. Getting quality ingredients does require some conscious decision as natural foods are hard to get and expensive too. You may need to do firsthand research on where real foods can be obtained or buy organic produce straight from the farms. You could even rear your own poultry or grow your own crops to get your organic produce.

9. You do not drink green tea

Green tea is a healthy option for losing weight, as it has the ability to stabilize fats. You can utilize green tea in combination with resistance training to double your potential for fat loss. To add flavor to green tea, squeeze in some lemon to also boost the antioxidant properties of the health drink.

10. You are not exercising well

Exercise can help you improve your metabolic health and raise your confidence as well as improve your muscle tone. That said, despite the fact that exercising is necessary for weight loss, the calories burned are very minimal and can easily be replaced by the next meal you take.

So what should you do?

One trick here is to try lifting some weights, as this in turn helps you improve your muscle tone and lose weight eventually. Train in high intensity intervals to increase your human growth hormone levels, and then do some low intensity activities such as walking.

To help you exercise better, here is a 4-week training program that goes well with the Paleo diet and that can be practiced almost everywhere.

4-Week Workout Plan

Be aware that during the first week of working out, it's highly likely that you'll lose water weight so the actual weight loss will occur 2-4 weeks later. Within 3-4 weeks of regular exercise, men should lose about 8-12 pounds while women will lose 5-10 pounds. The workout provided here is for beginners and is comprised of easy to do daily exercises.

Week 1

1. Walk about 10,000 steps each day on an empty stomach, which should translate to 30 minutes of walking. To track your progress, buy a pedometer as this can help you determine the steps you take daily. Hitting that target translates to over 5 miles depending on the length of your strides.

2. Do around 20 wall push-ups. Furthermore, you can do this *"Monkey push"* pose to help strengthen the back, abdominal, arms and shoulders:

-Go into the 'up' posture of a push-up pose with your hands being directly below the shoulders and the body in a straight line, from the head to toe

-Keep the core tight and then push through your toes and hop forward, ensuring that you land slowly with your feet on the outside of your hands.

-Then hop back into your initial position

-Bend your elbows as you keep them close to the body in order to lower your body towards the floor

-Finally push back up to complete 1 rep and then repeat for 10-12 reps.

3. Have a 5-minute session where you can walk for a minute for warm-up, then do knee bends for another minute. Follow this with a minute each for push-ups and sit-ups and then a minute of walking to cool down.

4. One day during the week, reserve 30 minutes to do intense cardio, where you can try out swimming, biking, skating or walking/jogging on a treadmill.

Week 2

1. Aim to take 10, 000 steps daily, which should comprise of 30 minutes of walking, on empty stomach

2. Do about 25 wall-pushups or the "monkey push"

3. Practice a 10 minute daily session that comprises of the following workouts:

- 1 min walking to warm-up

- 20 jumping jacks

- 1 min crouching jumps

- 20 jumps forward and backwards

- 1 min normal-paced walking in place

- 20 one-legged hops

- 20 side jumps: jump over a broom from right to left and then from left to right

- 1 minute fast walking in place

- 1 min relaxing walking in place

4. Also have a session of 45 minutes for more intense cardio like roller skating or biking, or instead enroll in a fitness class.

Week 3

1. Aim to take 10, 000 steps daily, which should comprise of 30 minutes of walking, on empty stomach

2. Perform 30 wall pushups

3. Dedicate a 12-15 minutes session to practice the following workouts:

- 1 min walking in place

- 2 min fast walking in place

- 1 min jumping in place

- 1 min knee bends

- 1 min walking in place

- 1 min side sit-ups

- 1 min *"modified" plank pose*

-Start at a push-up pose and then bend your elbows down as far as possible, and straighten them

-Now lift the hips while you push back into downward dog posture; as you press your heels towards the floor

-Return to plank pose and repeat the pose 10 times.

-The exercise is meant to target your shoulders, triceps, biceps and upper body

- 1 min stretching

- 1 min fast walking in place

- 2 min of breathing exercises

-For breathing exercises, just stand at upright position and then breathe in as you raise your arms above your head.

-Then exhale as you keep the legs straight. Now bend forward at your waist until you feel a stretch in the legs.

-Repeat the breathing exercise 4 times.

4. During this week, try 45 minutes intense cardio on one day.

Week 4

1. Do your usual 10, 00 steps and 30 minutes' walk when hungry

2. Do at least 40 wall push-ups

3. Have an at least 15 minute session to do these exercises:

- 1 min walking in place

- 20 jumps from right to left and then left to right

- 1 min push-ups

- 20 jumping jacks

- 1 min walking in place

- 20 jumping jacks

- 1 min sit-ups

- 1 min knee bends

- 20 jumps in the air

- 2 min lunges. You can try this *hip flexor lunge stretch.*

-Begin at lunge pose on the floor, with your right foot forward and the left knee back. The knees should be about 90 degrees.

-Ensure your torso is straight and engage the abs. Then lunge forward, and press gently until you experience a stretch in the hip's front.

-Now squeeze your glutes to perform a deeper stretch. Hold the pose for 30 seconds before switching sides.

- 2 minutes very fast walking, followed by 1 minute normal working

- 1 min "sun salutations"

-Be at an upright position then breathe in as you raise hands above your head. Ensure that you stretch to the maximum

-Exhale gently as you lower your arms to touch your toes.

4. Also include one 1-hour session of intensive cardio to maximize weight loss.

As you exercise to lose weight, these 5 steps can help you:

1. **Do shorter workouts**

Overworking only leaves you fatigued and depressed, and may not be effective at all. Instead, choose to practice short but intense workouts, which can burn more calories in a few minutes. You can start with a

10-15 minute workout session of intense cardio and then watch the results.

2. Do not skip workouts

Workouts helps in breaking down calories so ensure you don't skip the gym or aerobic exercises. Set an alarm to remind you of your evening workout to ensure you achieve the extra boost of endorphins that comes from working out. If late from a meeting or if it's dark outside, do a couple of indoor exercises such as sit-ups, crunches, flutter kicks or planks.

3. Keep moving

Weight is easily lost through workouts and reducing caloric intake. Even when you don't hit the gym, you can significantly burn calories by moving around; walking to a meeting, taking the stairs or parking your car away far from the grocery store doors.

4. Do intense cardio

To boost your metabolism easily, do a 45-minute cardio session daily as this can elevate your metabolism even after you stop sweating. This is an excellent post-workout strategy you can practice almost everywhere. Try interval training such as the pyramid treadmill workout, indoor cycling, running or swimming.

5. Try HIIT workouts

Also referred to as High-intensity interval training, this strategy combines intense activity together with periods of moderate-to-low effort. This type of interval training can burn more calories and also boost the metabolism more effectively as opposed to steady workouts. Furthermore, you can easily complete high intensity training in a shorter time.

For those who are professional athletes, you may need a stronger exercising regime along with a dieting plan that supports your muscles. When it comes to working out for both body-builders and professional athletes, this diet can support your need for calories as well as the concept of healthy dieting. However, body builders and athletes require hour after hour of sustained energy production for workouts and need to achieve quick recovery after exercise. Thus, there's a need to create a modified Paleo Diet specifically for Athletes. Such a diet can help athletes to combine high glycemic foods with low-carb foods in order to endure sports or challenging workouts. For this reason, a few 'un-allowed' foods are allowed but on a limited basis; or based on daily eating stages relative to exercising. Let's see how that works:

Paleo for Bodybuilders and Athletes

To help you build muscle without starving or having to over-indulge, it's recommended that you follow the Paleo diet in a few phases. Have about four stages where you eat based on your current level of training, just like this:

Stage 1: Eating before exercise

Athletes should eat carbs that range from low to moderate glycemic index about 2 hours before long workouts or sporting activity. The food has to have sufficient proteins and fats, but ought to be low in fiber.

In this case, you should consume around 200-300 calories each hour before the exercising period begins. If it's harder to eat 2 hours before exercise, then you can eat around 200 calories 10 minutes before exercise. A simple diet to adopt is a pre-workout breakfast smoothie made of almond butter, egg white protein powder, banana and 8 ounces of brewed natural decaf green tea. Whiz these in the food processor and serve with baked yam.

Stage 2: Eating during exercise

You need to consume high glycemic index carbs, preferably those in liquid form, during workouts. You can reach for sports drinks if working out for longer periods or drink plain water for those that take less than one hour. Basically, you need to consume 200-400 calories during exercise and this depends on your body size, nature of exercise and your experience.

Stage 3: Eating after exercise

Around 30 minutes post workout, you should consume a recovery drink that is comprised of proteins and carbs in the ratio of 1:4. For instance, you can blend 3 tablespoons of protein powder, 3-5 tablespoons of glucose, 1 banana, 2 pinches of salt and 16 ounces of fruit juice.

Alternatively, you can prepare a homemade brew that comprises of glucose, protein powder, egg white protein powder and cantaloupe. Also eat raisins as these help restore your body's alkalinity while recovering. You need to prioritize this 30 minute window to facilitate recovery.

Stage 4: Eating for extended recovery

A few hours after exercise, continue to focus your diet on moderate to high glycemic index carbohydrates. Here, you need to consider a 4-5:1 carb to protein ratio and so it's time to eat glucose-rich foods, which help sustain the recovery process. Eat foods such as cauliflower rice, quinoa, yams, sweet potatoes, raisins and other complex carbs. Then for the remainder of your day, you can focus on optimal Paleo foods such as fruits, veggies and lean meats until you get back to stage 1.

Bottom line:

The rule of the thumb in Paleo diet for athletes is to eat in stages. During most of your meals, follow the Paleo diet as it's supposed to be followed; but right before exercise, while exercising and a few hours after exercise, adjust the diet as required. There are 8 principals of the Paleo diet for athletes:

1. Only consume whole and natural foods as opposed to processed varieties.

2. Add plenty of veggies, fruits and nuts; and moderate intake of refined sugars and grains.

3. Boost intake of lean proteins from sources such as game meats, lean cuts of red meat, fish and poultry.

4. Increase consumption of omega 3 fatty acids from walnuts, fatty fish, avocadoes, eggs and other healthy sources.

5. Ditch any trans-fats and moderate your intake of saturated foods that come from baked goods, hard margarine, fried foods, and processed snack foods.

6. Choose polyunsaturated and monounsaturated fats such as olive oil instead of saturated fats.

7. Do not eat processed meats like deli meats, sausage and bacon as well as high-fat dairy products.

8. Adopt water as your main drink especially during and after exercises.

How Much Macro-Nutrients do You Need?

The dietary requirement for proteins, carbs and fats depends on your training season. That said, you need to maintain a constant protein intake all year round; let's say at a range of 20-25% of your total daily caloric intake. Though this is contrary to what our ancestors ate, it's advisable to reduce protein intake in favor of high carb diet.

But why is it so?

It's a fact that athletes need a high protein diet but it's carbs and not proteins that are used to generate workout fuel. You need protein just for building muscles and growth of body cells, your protein requirement would still revolve at 1.2-2.2 grams/kg of body weight. If in doubt, this study confirms that even experienced strength athletes can sustain muscles within this range.

So how should you balance carbs and fat intake as you transit from period of no-exercise to high intensity exercise? Before exercise, ensure that 30 percent of the calories you eat come from fats and the remaining 50 percent from complex carbs. And during high intensity exercise, boost carb intake to around 60 percent to cater to the increasing demand for body fuel. Your fat intake should be around 20 percent more or less as the protein is consumed. But during periods where training is greatly reduced you should get back to traditional Paleo foods to prevent possible weight gain. The diet plan should comprise of mainly non-starchy veggies, low-carb fruits such as berries, lean meats and a moderate amount of nuts.

Here are a list of foods that can make you live strong, lean, and paleo.

- ***Organic free-range eggs***

Eggs are not just eggs as far as Paleo lifestyle is concerned. If you wish to get healthy sources of omega-3 fatty acids and proteins, reach for eggs from free-range chicken as opposed to the conventional farm raised ones. These organic eggs have a similar feel to those the cavemen ate and remained healthy in the wild. You need to do away with those egg beaters or other substitutes for eggs and adopt the organic form.

- **Sweet potatoes**

Ditch the starchy potatoes that are sold in form of mashed potatoes, potato chips and French fries, but instead use sweet potatoes. Replacing potatoes shouldn't be a challenge as sweet potato can cook mashed and chips potatoes, potato hash along with French fries and other delicacies.

Cauliflower is a good replacement for mashed potatoes as it has almost similar appearance and tastes as great. For healthier carb sources, try yams, cauliflower rice and kale chips to replace ordinary potatoes.

- **Paleo bread**

Regular bread is not approved in Paleo diet, though you can make your own bread from approved ingredients. To make your healthy bread, all you require is coconut flour, almond flour and other substitutes. You can make zucchini bread, banana bread, pumpkin bread and coconut bread. Try mixing coconut and almond flour to create homemade flour that suites all baking applications.

- **Dark chocolate**

This is a good post workout snack, which is rich in antioxidants. Also, try cocoa powder that has no added sugars or other sweeteners. However, don't take milk chocolate; chocolate chips are only allowed if they are soy and dairy-free.

The Paleo diet is effective when applied appropriately without cheating, skipping meals or giving up at any stage of dieting. For that reason, you'll need to make a dieting plan that you can easily commit to. In the next section, we shall look at how to get started on a Paleo diet for the first 4 weeks of your diet. You can tweak any of these meals with any of the ingredients on the grocery list here to make the meals as flexible, adventurous, or as flavorful as you want. Here is the sample meal plan:

4-Week Meal Plan

Week 1

Day 1

Breakfast

1 cup coconut or almond milk

2 teaspoons maple syrup, sugar-free

2 slices pumpkin bread

1/2 cup mixed berries

Snack

1 cup cantaloupe melon

Lunch

Chicken & vegetable salad

Snack

1 medium orange

Dinner

Salmon with a salad & basil dressing

1/2 cup cooked quinoa

Day 2

Breakfast

Chicken-apple sausage

1 cup blueberries

1 cup coconut milk

Snacks

Handful almond nuts

Lunch

Honey & orange roast sea bass with veggies

1 tablespoon vinegar & oil salad dressing

6 ounces vanilla coconut yogurt

Snacks

Candied macadamia nuts

Dinner

Beef tenderloin with Brussels sprouts

1 cup watermelon

3/4 cup cooked quinoa

Day 3

Breakfast

Mushroom & cauliflower rice frittata

1 cup nut milk

Snack

1 small banana

Lunch

Chicken & veggie salad

1 medium apple

Snack

1 Apricot

Dinner

Broccoli parmesan meatballs

1 cup zucchini "noodles"

1/2 cup steamed carrots

1 cup strawberries

Day 4

Breakfast

Eggs benedict with zucchini pancakes

Green smoothie

Snack

1 small apple

Lunch

Grain-free pizza

1/2 cup papaya

Snack

1 slice rice bread

1 teaspoon creamy nut butter

Dinner

1/2 cup cooked quinoa

4 ounces grilled scallops

1/2 cup sautéed yellow and red peppers with thinly sliced onion: just sauté the bell pepper strips with red onion and a teaspoon olive oil.

½ teaspoon dried basil to sprinkle on the veggies

1/2 cup sliced grapes

Day 5

Breakfast

2 slices Paleo-friendly bread

1 teaspoon nut butter

1 cup green tea

1/2 small banana

Snack

1 handful mixed nuts

Lunch

Tuna pocket: made with 3 ounces canned tuna mixed with 2 tablespoons each grated carrot, celery and minced onion

1 cup mixed berries

Snack

Candied pecans

Dinner

1 cup romaine lettuce, red peppers and carrots tossed with 2 tablespoons dressing

1/2 cup baked sweet potato

3 ounces lean grilled flank steak

1/2 baked pear; dressed with low-calorie cranberry juice and baked in oven for 30 to 40 minutes at 375 degrees

Day 6

Breakfast

1 cup almond milk

1/2 cup blueberries

1 small wheat-free muffin

Snack

1/2 avocado seasoned with pepper and salt

Lunch

Honey & orange roast sea bass

Creamy chopped cauliflower salad

1 cup strawberries

Snack

1 hard-boiled egg seasoned with pepper and salt

Dinner

Salmon with salad & basil dressing

1/2 baked sweet potato

Day 7

Breakfast

Scrambled eggs

1 cup coconut milk

Snack

2 tablespoons hummus

1-2 slices pumpkin bread

Lunch

Broccoli parmesan meatballs

1 cup tossed salad mix

1 tablespoon citrus dressing

Sliced tomatoes with pesto drizzle

Snack

4 ounces baby carrots

Dinner

1/2 cup mixed cantaloupe chunks and honeydew

1/2 cup stir-fried red bell pepper and broccoli, stir-fry
the veggies over high heat in 1 teaspoon canola oil

8 ounces grilled Cornish game hen

Week 2

Day 1

Breakfast

Small palm-sized portion of macadamia nuts

Decaffeinated coffee

Snack

Smoked pork

Homemade curried carrot soup

Lunch

Sauerkraut

Brown mustard

2 uncured hot dogs

Snack

2 hardboiled eggs

Dinner

Pureed cauliflower "rice"

Beef & broccoli with coconut aminos

Day 2

Breakfast

2 medium eggs cooked in bacon fat

1 banana

Snack

1 handful nuts

Lunch

Smoked pork over green salad with carrots

Homemade dijon vinaigrette

Snack

Raw hazelnuts, broiled with tablespoon each of cocoa powder and coconut oil

Dinner

Meatball salad with canned tomatoes

Black olives and fresh basil

Day 3

Breakfast

Spinach frittata

Snack

Canned tuna with ¼ cup avocado (substitute for mayonnaise)

Lunch

Beef and broccoli stir-fry

Dinner

Organ Meat Pie, made with ground beef, beef liver, carrots, broccoli and cauliflower puree.

Day 4

Breakfast

Mushroom frittata

Snack

Buffalo jerky stick

Lunch

Leftover organ meat pie

1 cup pineapple cubes

Snack

1/3 cup roasted, salted almonds

Dinner

1/2 cup low-fat frozen yogurt, sugar-free

1 cup raw spinach tossed with 1 teaspoon champagne vinegar and 2 teaspoons olive oil

½ cup cauliflower 'couscous'

3 ounces cod, baked

Day 5

Breakfast

Spinach and bacon

2 fried eggs

Snack

1 slice pineapple

Lunch

Tuna salad with homemade mayo

1 cup dairy-free yogurt

Snack

1 handful walnuts

Dinner

Grilled salmon with zucchini "noodles" and some sautéed vegetables

Day 6

Breakfast

Scrambled eggs with green smoothie

Snack

1 apple

Lunch

1/3 chicken breast with dressing

Green salad

Snack

Candied pecans

Dinner

Grilled salmon with sautéed vegetables

Day 7

Breakfast

Egg salad

1 cup dairy-free milk

Snack

Celery sticks with hummus

Lunch

1/2 cup cauliflower

Grilled chicken with spinach

Snack

1 cup mango cubes

Dinner

Green salad

Sliced flank steak

Drizzled balsamic vinegar

Week 3

Day 1

Breakfast

1 cup dairy free milk

2 teaspoons maple syrup, sugar-free

1/2 cup mixed berries

2 grain-free pancakes, about 4-inch

Snack

Some baby carrots

Lunch

Steamed broccoli

1 cup cooked Quinoa

Chicken breast cooked in olive oil

Snack

10 cashews

Dinner

180g chicken

Cooked red cabbage and pan-seared spinach

Lemon juice for flavor

Day 2

Breakfast

Smoothie made of;

70g plain yoghurt

30g blueberries

5 strawberries

1 peeled and sliced orange

Snack

¼ avocado

Lunch

Previous night's leftovers

Snack

30g hummus

Carrot sticks

Dinner

Grilled green vegetables and 10g tofu

1/2 cup cauliflower rice

Day 3

Breakfast

Poached egg on a slice of sourdough toast topped with 1 tomato diced

Green smoothie

Snack

1 orange

Lunch

Herbed chicken soup with spring vegetables

1 (one-ounce) grain-free roll

1 small apple

Snack

Banana Strawberry Shake 60ml

Dinner

3-ounce wild caught salmon

Veggie salad with lettuce, spinach and basil dressed in vinaigrette and seasoned with salt and pepper

Day 4

Breakfast

1/2 cup coconut milk

1 ounce grain-free breakfast muffin

1/2 broiled grapefruit

Snack

10 cashews

Lunch

15ml vinaigrette for flavor

180g baked chicken

Iceberg lettuce and spinach together with chopped carrots, 30g diced walnuts, 30g cranberries and spring onions drizzled with 15ml vinaigrette

Snack

1/2 cup cooked edamame

Dinner

200g grilled trout with skillet-roasted orange, red, and yellow capsicums.

Day 5

Breakfast

1-cup coconut milk

2 slices sourdough toast with honey

Snack

1 banana

Lunch

300ml miso soup

1 grain-free roll

Snack

5 Brazil nuts

Dinner

1-cup cauliflower rice and steamed broccoli

180g grilled chicken drizzled with lemon juice

Day 6

Breakfast

1 slice sourdough toast with avocado

1-cup fresh fruit juice

Snack

30g hummus

Celery sticks

Lunch

Previous night's leftovers

Snack

Green smoothie

Dinner

95g canned tuna on a bed of spinach, olives, carrots, and spring greens

Season with black pepper and Celtic salt

Day 7

Breakfast

3 eggs, scrambled with green pepper

Coconut cream

2 slices of bacon

Snack

10 cashews

Lunch

Warm Chicken salad with Quinoa & Pomegranate

Snack

1 medium sized banana

Dinner

200 g baked salmon on a bed of spring greens, red cabbage, and baby spinach drizzled 30ml lemon juice

Week 4

Day 1

Breakfast

1 poached egg

2 sliced of grain-free bread

1 cup almond milk

Snack

4 walnuts

Lunch

3 ounces lean protein, e.g. turkey or tuna

2 slices grain-free bread

Lettuce, tomato

Mustard

Snack

6 almonds, slivered

Dinner

5 ounces grilled salmon with teriyaki sauce

1 cup steamed broccoli drizzled with vinegar

1 medium sized sweet potato

Day 2

Breakfast

1 cup coconut or almond milk

2 teaspoons sugar-free jam

1 small zucchini bread, toasted

1/2 cup mixed fruits such as papaya cubes, kiwi, and pineapple

Snack

12 almonds

Lunch

1 large slice pizza; grain-free with veggies

Snack

¼ cup unsweetened dairy-free yogurt

Dinner

1 cup steamed vegetables with some avocado

6 ounces fish, poultry, or lean meat

Day 3

Breakfast

Smoothie with mixed berries, apple, and banana

Snack

6 cashews

Lunch

1 small grain-free roll

2-4 tablespoons low-fat dressing

4 ounces shrimp

1 cups veggie salad drizzled 2-4 tablespoons low fat dressing

Snack

12 ounces tomato juice, low-sodium

Dinner

A large Salad

2 tablespoons light dressing

4 ounces of chicken

1 fruit

Day 4

Breakfast

1 cup non-dairy milk

2 teaspoons maple syrup, sugar-free

1/2 cup mixed berries

2 no-grain pancakes, about 4-inch

Snack

12 almonds

Lunch

2 slices tomato

2 ounces turkey, tuna, salmon

2 slices rye bread

Snack

Roasted pumpkin seeds

Dinner

5 ounces fish or poultry grilled with spices

Salad with 2 tablespoons light dressing

1 slice grain-free bread

1-2 teaspoons olive oil for bread

10 low-sodium black olives

Day 5

Breakfast

2 eggs, fried

2 pieces cooked bacon

1 apple

Snack

1 fruit

Lunch

Sandwich of;

2 slices grain-free bread

Lettuce and tomato

1 tablespoon homemade mayonnaise

2 ounces shrimp or chicken salad

Snack

12 almonds

Dinner

½ cup cooked cauliflower rice

4 ounces fish, poultry, or lean meat

1 cup green vegetables

Day 6

Breakfast

2 eggs, fried with butter

Mushrooms or green peppers

Snack

3 dried apricots

Lunch

3 ounces chicken

Large salad drizzled with 1 tablespoon olive oil and vinegar

Snack

Celery sticks and hummus

Dinner

4 ounces shrimp grilled or baked with spices

½ cup cauliflower "rice"

1 cup steamed veggies

Day 7

Breakfast

3 eggs, scrambled with green pepper

2 slices of bacon

Snack

30g hummus

Carrot sticks

Lunch

2 ounces turkey, chicken

2 slices grain-free bread

Lettuce, tomato

1 tablespoon sugar-free dressing

Snack

10 cashews

Dinner

1 small sweet potato

1 cup sautéed green vegetables

4 ounces shrimp, sautéed with olive oil

Let's even take it further by discussing some delicious Paleo friendly recipes that you can prepare.

Delicious Paleo Recipes

Here are amazing delicious Paleo recipes for your experimentation pleasure

Breakfast Recipes

1: Portobello Breakfast Bakes

Serves 2

Ingredients

2 tablespoons parsley, chopped

4 slices of bacon

2-4 large eggs

2 Portobello mushroom caps

1 tablespoon of coconut oil or olive oil

Salt & pepper

Directions

1. Preheat your oven to 400 degrees F and then use coconut or olive oil to lightly grease a baking dish.

2. Using a knife, remove the stems from mushrooms to create a small bowl shape.

3. Place the mushroom cups in the baking dish with the right side up and bake for about 5 minutes. Flip upside down and then bake for another 5 minutes.

4. Meanwhile, prepare the bacon. Use aluminum foil to line a baking sheet and then position the bacon strips in a single layer on the baking sheet. Bake the bacon for 10-15 minutes until done.

5. Remove the caps from the oven and then crack 1-2 eggs into each; return the mushrooms and eggs into the oven.

6. Bake these for an additional 10-15 minutes for the egg whites and yolks to cook as desired.

7. Let the bacon cool down before cutting it into bite size pieces. To serve, sprinkle the eggs with parsley and bacon bits.

2: Breakfast Muffins

Serves 4

Ingredients

2 cups of banana

½ cup of coconut milk, unsweetened

¼ cup of coconut oil

1 cup of sliced strawberries, frozen

2 teaspoons of maple syrup

1 tablespoon of flaxseed, ground

⅓ cup of almond flour

½ cup of dates

Directions

1. Line muffin tins with paper liners and then place ground flax, almond meal, and dates in a food processor. Pulse the mixture to make it crumbly, transfer to a bowl, and then stir in maple syrup. Gently press a tablespoon of the mixture into the bottom of the muffin tin to create a crust.

2. Place semi-thawed strawberries into a food processor and process to until smooth. Slowly add in

coconut and coconut milk until you achieve a thick, sorbet-like consistency.

3. Pour the strawberries into a bowl and gently fold in the bananas. Then divide the strawberry-banana mixture over the top of the crust evenly.

4. Put the muffin tin in the freezer and let it freeze and solidify. Once done, remove from the muffin tins and let the muffins thaw for 10 additional minutes before serving.

3: Avocado & Bacon Muffins

Makes 12

Ingredients

½ teaspoon of baking soda

½ cup of coconut flour

1 cup of coconut milk

2 cups of avocado

4 eggs

6 short cut bacon rashers

1 small onion

Salt & pepper

Directions

1. Preheat the oven to 350 degrees F and then use coconut oil to grease 12 muffin cups.

2. Finely dice the bacon and onion and then brown them in a pan.

3. Meanwhile, use a fork to mix the eggs and avocado and then stir in the milk.

4. Add in salt and pepper, baking soda, and coconut flour and mix well to break up all lumps.

5. Fold in 3 quarters of the onion and cooked bacon mixture.

6. Divide the mixture between the 12 muffin cups and top with the reserved onion and bacon.

7. Bake the cups in the preheated oven for about 20 minutes and allow them to cool before you remove the muffins from the cups.

8. Serve immediately or alternatively keep chilled in the fridge for outdoor breakfasts.

4: Ham and Egg Cups

Serves 2-4

Ingredients

4 large eggs

4 slices ham

Fresh parsley, basil, and scallions

Salt and pepper, to taste

Nonstick cooking spray

Directions

1. Preheat your oven to about 400 degrees F. Meanwhile, use a non-stick cooking spray to lightly coat 4 muffin cups.

2. In each muffin cup, fit a slice of ham and then crack an egg in each cup.

3. Bake in the oven until the egg whites cook but the egg yolks are still runny. This should take around 13 minutes.

4. You can season the eggs with pepper and salt and carefully remove the eggcups.

5. Sprinkle the dish with chopped parsley, scallions, or with basil.

5: Baked Squash & Eggs

Serves 1

Ingredients

1 small to medium egg

¼ teaspoon of dried thyme

1 tablespoon of fresh, chopped flat leaf parsley

1 star squash

Directions

1. Remove the tops from your star squashes and hollow out a bit of the insides to create room for the egg and spices.

2. Sprinkle with dried thyme and parsley. Now crack the egg and add it to the squash.

3. Bake at 350 degrees F until the eggs set, which should take about 30 minutes.

6: Paleo Ham Stir-Fry

Serves 4

Ingredients

1 medium avocado, diced

¼ teaspoon of black pepper, ground

½ pound of ham, diced

1/8 teaspoon of thyme

1 small sweet potato, diced

4 medium mushrooms, sliced

¼ medium yellow onion, diced

1 tablespoon of coconut oil

Directions

1. Heat a large sauté pan over medium heat, and then add in coconut oil. Add in thyme, sweet potatoes, mushrooms, and onions.

2. Cook until the sweet potatoes are tender, making sure to stir regularly.

3. Add in a few drops of water to the pan, cover and continue cooking.

4. Toss in the ham and cook until heated through and then season with fresh ground pepper.

5. Top with an avocado and serve. Enjoy!

7: Chicken and Apple Sausage

Serves 2-4

Ingredients

2 teaspoons of garlic powder

1 tablespoon of fresh oregano, finely chopped

3 tablespoons of fresh parsley, finely chopped

1 tablespoon of fresh thyme leaves, finely chopped

1 apple, peeled and finely diced

1 pound of ground chicken or 2 large chicken breasts

Coconut oil

Salt and pepper

Directions

1. Begin by preheating the oven to 425 degrees F, and then in a skillet, melt 3 tablespoons of coconut oil.

2. Over medium-high heat, cook oregano, parsley, thyme, and apples for about 7-8 minutes, or until soft. Cool for 5 minutes.

3. If using chicken breast, process it and then mix the chicken with the rest of the ingredients in the skillet.

4. From the mixture, form 12 ½-inch-thick patties and position them on a baking tray lined with foil.

5. Bake the patties at 170 degrees F for about 20 minutes and then cool.

6. If you need the sausages browned, pan-fry in coconut oil or alternatively, pan fry raw sausages instead of baking.

7. Store in the freezer or fridge and reheat in the morning in a microwave or skillet.

8: Paleo Breakfast Burger

Serves 4

Ingredients

8 slices of cooked bacon

½-cup of ground sausage

5 eggs

2 tablespoons of almond meal

1 pound of beef, ground

2 teaspoons of basil

1 teaspoon of garlic, minced

2-3 sundried tomatoes, sliced

Directions

1. Combine the beef with one egg, sun dried tomatoes, almond meal, garlic, and basil; form into 4 burger patties.

2. Cook bacon, drain, and set aside.

3. In a skillet, cook burger patties for 5 minutes on each side and set them on plates.

4. Once done, fry sausage in skillet and top your burgers with sausage and bacon.

5. Finally fry the 4 eggs one at a time and place them on top of burgers. Serve and enjoy.

9: Pumpkin Waffles

Serves 5

Ingredients

1 teaspoon of vanilla extract

1 teaspoon of baking powder

NOTE: Do not use commercial baking powder because it contains gluten, cornstarch, and aluminum, none of which is Paleo-friendly. Make your own Paleo-friendly baking powder (1 tablespoon) by mixing 1 teaspoon of baking soda with 2 parts cream of tartar).

1 teaspoon of baking soda

2 tablespoons of pumpkin pie spice

½ cup of coconut flour

¼ cup of melted coconut oil,

½ cup of almond butter

5 large eggs

½ cup of pumpkin puree

2 large bananas, mashed

Maple syrup, for serving

Pinch of fine-grain sea salt

Directions

1. Start by preheating the waffle iron

2. Meanwhile, mix together bananas, coconut oil, almond butter, eggs, and pumpkin puree in a food processor or blender. Combine and fully blend the ingredients.

3. When smooth, add in vanilla, baking powder, baking soda, pumpkin pie spice, coconut flour, and salt, and continue to mix until blended.

4. Lightly brown the waffle iron using some melted coconut oil. Using your waffle maker's guidelines for suggested milliliter quantity, ladle the batter into your already hot and greased waffle maker.

5. Spread the batter evenly along the surface while ensuring you leave about a half-inch border.

5. Follow the manufacturer's instructions to cook the waffles until done. Then set aside on your plate. Keep warm as you prepare other waffles.

10: Granola with Oven-dried Strawberries

Serves 6

Ingredients

2/3 cup of chia seeds

2/3 cup of dried goji berries

2/3 cup of dried cranberries

6 dried apricots

10 medium strawberries

1 ½ cup of coconut flakes

2 cups of macadamia nuts

2 ½ cups of raw almonds

Directions

1. First wash and pat dry the strawberries. Slice each of the strawberries into 5-6 slices. Preheat the oven to 165 degrees F.

2. Place your sliced strawberries on a tray or rack that has holes and then bake for 2-3 hours. After 2 hours, peel and turn your slices over.

3. Remove from heat and set aside to cool; increase the heat to 300 degrees F.

4. Mix the macadamia nuts and almonds in a large baking tray, and roast them for around 10 minutes. Stir the mixture at 1-2 minute intervals. When browned remove from heat and cool the nuts in a bowl.

5. At this point, scatter coconut flakes into the baking tray and roast them while stirring until golden brown.

6. After about 3-4 minutes, remove from heat and cool. Grind some macadamia nuts and almonds in a food processor, into small crumbs.

7. At this point, dice the dried apricots. Now combine the strawberries, apricots, coconut flakes, nuts, and the remaining ingredients and allow them to cool completely.

8. You can serve immediately or store the granola in an airtight container for a few weeks.

11: Spinach and Chorizo Frittata

Serves 2

Ingredients

2 heaping cups of fresh spinach, coarsely chopped

½ pound of fresh chorizo or spicy Italian sausage

¼ sweet onion, chopped

2 tablespoons of olive oil

Unrefined sea salt and pepper

¾ cup of grated vegan cheese

½ cup of almond milk

12 eggs, pastured.

Directions

1. Combine milk and eggs in a medium bowl, and whisk. Add in ½ cup of cheese, season with pepper and salt, and then set aside.

2. Heat the oil in a large pan over medium heat, and then add onions and chorizo.

3. Cook until the chorizo is browned and the onions look translucent, about 6-8 minutes, ensuring you stir from time to time.

4. Add spinach and cook for another 6 minutes until wilted. Reduce the heat and pour the egg mixture into the pan on top of the veggies and meat.

5. Cook on low for about 15 minutes or until the edges of the frittata set. Sprinkle the remaining ¼ cup of cheese and broil for about 4 minutes.

6. Once the center is set and the top turns golden brown, allow the frittata to chill for a few minutes.

7. When ready, the edges should pull away from the sides of the skillet to make serving easier.

12: Breakfast Casserole

Serves 5-6

Ingredients

½ teaspoon of garlic powder

½ teaspoon of sea salt

10 free-range eggs, whisked

2 cups of spinach, chopped

½ yellow onion, diced

1½ pound of breakfast sausage

½ teaspoon of fine sea salt

1 large sweet potato or yam, diced

2 tablespoons of coconut oil, melted

Directions

1. First, pre-heat your oven to 400 degrees F as you grease a 9×12 baking dish.

2. Toss the diced sweet potatoes in the oil and sprinkle sea salt.

3. Place the sweet potatoes onto the baking sheet and then bake for around 20-25 minutes, until tender.

4. As your sweet potatoes cook, heat a big sauté pan over medium heat and then add in breakfast sausage along with yellow onion. Cook through.

5. Put the meat mixture in the baking dish and then add in spinach, sweet potatoes and eggs, and season with sea salt and garlic powder. Combine fully.

6. Finally, place in the oven and bake for around 25-30 minutes until the eggs are set in the middle.

13: Paleo Breakfast Bars

Makes 16

Ingredients

¼ cup of raisins

¼ cup slivered almonds, blanched

½ cup sunflower seeds

½ cup of pumpkin seeds

½ cup of shredded coconut, unsweetened

1 teaspoon of vanilla extract

1 tablespoon of water

2 tablespoons honey

¼ cup of coconut oil

¼ teaspoon of Celtic sea salt

1 cup of blanched almond flour

Directions

1. Mix the salt and almond floor in a food processor and then pulse in water, honey, coconut oil, and vanilla extract.

2. Follow with the raisins, almond slivers, sunflower seeds, pumpkin seeds, and the coconut.

3. Press the dough into an 8×8 baking dish and wet your hands to help pat the dough down.

4. Bake the dough at 350 F for around 30 minutes. Once ready, cut into squares and serve.

14: Eggs with Braised Spinach

Serves 2

Ingredients

1 tablespoon of olive oil

¼ cup of sliced organic bacon

1 cup of fresh baby spinach

½ small red onion

2 rings of large green pepper

2 large eggs

Salt & Pepper

Directions

1. Slice the bell peppers in two 1-inch thick slices near the center (in a way that will create a ring). Reserve the rest.

2. Using the oil, grease a non-stick pan and then cook pepper rings on one side for 3 minutes.

3. In each bell pepper ring, crack an egg and then season with salt and pepper. Cook until the egg white is firm.

4. Warm the remaining olive oil in a separate pan then add in chopped onion. Cook until slightly brown.

5. Add the sliced bacon and cook for a few seconds. Add drained baby spinach then season with salt.

6. Cook for 1 minute and then serve.

15: Paleo Scramble

Serves 1

Ingredients

2 tablespoons of coconut oil

2 radishes grated

1 pinch of cayenne pepper

1 tablespoon of turmeric

1 small clove garlic, minced

2 kale leaves, shredded

2 pastured eggs

Optional: Radish and clover sprouts

Directions

1. Heat a pan and lightly sauté garlic in coconut oil.

2. Crack eggs and cook them until scrambled.

3. Once almost ready, add in turmeric, shredded kale, and cayenne.

4. If desired, top with the sprouts and radish and enjoy

16: Buttered Eggs

Serves 2

Ingredients

4 organic eggs

½ cup of fresh parsley, chopped

½ cup of fresh cilantro, chopped

½ teaspoon of sea salt

1 teaspoon of fresh thyme leaves

2 garlic cloves, finely chopped

2 tablespoons of coconut oil

¼ teaspoon of ground cayenne

¼ teaspoon of ground cumin

Directions

1. Melt coconut oil in a non-stick skillet for 60 seconds.

2. Add chopped garlic and cook for 3 minutes on low heat. Once the garlic begins to brown, add thyme.

3. Brown for 30-60 seconds then add in parsley and cilantro. Cook on moderate heat until the thyme begins to crisp.

4. After around 3 minutes, add eggs in the pan. Crack them straight in without breaking the yolk.

5. Cover the pan, set the heat to low, and cook for 4-6 minutes. Once the yolks are set, serve.

17: Paleo Granola

Serves 6

Ingredients

2 teaspoons of nutmeg

2 teaspoons of cinnamon

¼ cup of hemp hearts

½ cup of coconut flakes

½ cup of walnuts

2 teaspoons of vanilla extract

1/3 cup of coconut oil

1½ cups of almond flour

Sea salt to taste

Directions

1. Preheat the oven to about 275 degrees Fahrenheit.

2. Combine all the ingredients in a large bowl, and mix well. You may consider melting coconut oil before adding to the other ingredients.

3. Spread the mixture onto a flat layer of a greased baking sheet and bake for about 40-50 minutes until the mixture has toasted.

4. Continue to mix after every 10 minutes or so in order for the contents to be fully and evenly baked.

5. Remove the baked granola from the oven and let it cool for a few minutes.

6. Divide the breakfast onto 4 plates and serve.

18: Amaranth porridge

Serves 2

Ingredients

1 medium pear, chopped

½ cup of blueberries or cranberries, dried

1 teaspoon of cinnamon

1 tablespoon of raw honey

¼ cup of hemp or pumpkin seeds

2 cups of filtered water

⅔ cup of whole-grain amaranth

Directions

1. In a skillet or a heavy 2-quart saucepan, mix amaranth and water. Ensure you stir the porridge constantly to prevent sticking.

2. Bring the amaranth-water mixture to a boil, cover and then lower the heat to simmer for around 25-30 minutes. Continue to stir at 10 minute intervals to ensure the grains do not stick to the pot. Cook until the water is fully absorbed.

3. Once done, remove the porridge from heat and then add in cinnamon, raw honey and the seeds and stir well.

4. Now divide the porridge between two bowls, or instead, keep a portion in a re-sealable container to serve next day. Top with pears and blueberries if you like.

19: Breakfast Salad

Serves 1-2

Ingredients

2 eggs

¼ teaspoon of sea salt

1 tablespoon of olive oil

¼ cup of pine nuts, toasted

1 small handful of parsley, chopped

1 small handful of fresh basil, chopped

1 avocado, diced

1 red pepper, diced

2 large handfuls of cherry tomatoes, halved

½ English cucumber, quartered and thickly sliced

2-3 tablespoons of olive oil for frying

Directions

1. In a large bowl, combine olive oil, pine nuts, all veggies and salt, and toss well.

2. Using medium heat, warm up a cast iron or a skillet and add a splash of oil. Once the pan is hot, add eggs

to the pan. You can add a splash of water to help cook eggs fast.

3. Once done, remove the eggs from the skillet and serve with the salad.

20: Eggs with Zucchini Pancakes

Serves 4

Ingredients

1 tablespoon of fresh, flat-leaf parsley, chopped

4 Zucchini Pancakes

4 slices of Canadian bacon

4 extra-large eggs, at room temperature

1 tablespoon of white vinegar

Directions

1. Preheat your oven to 275 degrees F. In a large and shallow saucepan, heat about 3 inches of water over medium heat until bubbles appear around the edges. Now add in the vinegar.

2. In a separate saucepan, heat 3 inches of water to a temperature of 130 degrees F. Once hot, remove from heat and cover.

3. Break each of the eggs at a time into a custard cup and then slide the eggs from the cup quickly into the barely simmering vinegar-water. Once you have added all the eggs, cook for about 2 minutes, or until the eggs become too lose.

4. Lift the eggs using a slotted spoon, each egg at a time, and then put them into the 130 degree F boiling water.

5. Cover the mixture and cook for around 15 minutes, while checking the temperatures of the water frequently to ensure its 130 degrees F. In case the temperature drops, add in boiling water to raise the temperature.

6. In a large non-stick frying pan placed over medium heat, place the Canadian bacon and fry it as you turn it regularly. Cook for 4 minutes to have it turn light brown around the edges.

7. Remove the meat from heat and put onto a baking sheet placed in a preheated oven to remain warm—if you haven't finished cooking the pancakes and eggs.

8. Place a warm pancake at the center of each plate and then top with a slice of bacon. Using the slotted spoon, lift the eggs from the water one at a time and use a kitchen towel to pat the excess water.

9. Put an egg atop the bacon. In case the eggs edges are rugged, use a small knife or kitchen knife to trim carefully.

10. On top of each egg, sprinkle about 3 tablespoons of hollandaise sauce and follow with chopped parsley. Serve the breakfast immediately.

21: Alkaline Breakfast

Serves 2

Ingredients

1 avocado

1 handful of broccoli florets

½ capsicum

2 large tomatoes or 12 cherry tomatoes

1 big handful of kale leaves

1 big handful of spinach leaves

50g uncooked quinoa

Black pepper

Himalayan salt

Juice of ½ lemon

Flax oil

Directions

1. Rinse the ½ cup of quinoa, and then place the quinoa and ¾ cup of water in a saucepan.

2. Bring the mixture to a boil and then set the heat to low for the quinoa to simmer covered. Once done, the

water should evaporate and the quinoa should have developed little curly tails.

3. Allow it cool down for a few minutes and then steam broccoli under a light steam for 5 minutes to make it crunchy.

4. Slice the avocados into cubes and slice the kale and spinach. Then slice the capsicum and halve the cherry tomatoes. If using cashew or almond nuts, also slice them up roughly or alternatively use the flat side of a knife to bash them.

5. After broccoli and quinoa are done, pour the dish into a large bowl and drizzle with lemon juice and olive oil. If desired, season then serve.

22: Spanish Frittata

Serves 4-6

Ingredients

1 cup of spinach or arugula

½ cup of sautéed mushrooms

1 small red onion, finely chopped

2 tablespoons of extra-virgin olive oil or coconut oil

½ teaspoon of sea salt

½ cup of coconut milk

12 large organic eggs

Directions

1. Preheat your oven to 375 degrees F. Meanwhile, whisk coconut milk, eggs, and 2 pinches of salt. Set the mixture aside.

2. Add coconut or extra virgin olive oil into a pan over medium heat. Once hot, sauté the onions for about 3 minutes or until translucent. Add in the mushrooms or other vegetable and sauté until soft.

3. Toss in the spinach and then fold into the veggie mixture to wilt. Once done, remove from the pan and set aside.

4. Lower the heat and add more coconut oil if needed. In the same skillet, add in the eggs and shake to distribute and then cook for 5 minutes over medium low heat.

5. Use a spatula to spread the eggs from edges to the center until the edges are no longer runny. Then arrange the vegetable mixture and top evenly.

6. At this point, move the mixture into an oven and cook for around 5 minutes or until lightly browned, and then remove from the oven.

7. Slide the cooked frittata partially onto a large plate, and place a plate over the pan using oven mitts. Then hold the plate and pan and invert them to make the frittata drop into the plate.

8. Slide the frittata into the pan with the partially cooked side facing up. Return in the oven and continue to cook for about 3-4 minutes, and then serve over a simple salad with a citrus vinaigrette.

Lunch Recipes

23: Pheasant and Wild Rice

Serves 4-6

Ingredients

1 large pheasant, halved (4 pounds)

½ pound of sliced fresh mushrooms

2 cups of uncooked wild rice

6 bacon strips, cut up

1 tablespoon of almond flour

1 teaspoon of pepper

1-½ teaspoons of paprika

2 teaspoons of dried oregano

2 teaspoons of garlic powder

2 teaspoons of salt

2-½ teaspoons of dried parsley flakes

3/4 cup of chopped onion

2-2/3 cups water

1 (10 3/4 ounces) can condensed-cream mushroom soup, undiluted

Directions

1. Combine condensed mushrooms, water, chopped onions, parsley flakes, garlic, dried oregano, paprika, salt and pepper, and bring the mixture to a boil.

2. In an oven bag, put your preferred Paleo-friendly flour while shaking to coat and place it in a 13x9 inches baking pan; add the bacon.

3. Sprinkle mushrooms and rice onto the bacon and pheasant, and pour the soup into a bag.

4. Cut about 6 half-an-inch slits in top of bag, and close the bag using a provided tie, before baking at 359 degrees F until a meat thermometer reads 180°.

5. After 1 to 1-1/2 hours, cool for 10 minutes and serve.

24: Garlic Shrimp

Serves 4

Ingredients

¼ cup of fresh parsley, chopped

¼ cup of chicken broth, fat-free

¼ cup of dry white wine

2 dozen jumbo raw shrimp, peeled, deveined

½ teaspoon of red pepper flakes

4 cloves garlic, peeled and crushed

2 tablespoons of olive oil

Pepper, freshly ground

Salt

Directions

1. Heat oil in a skillet over medium-high heat. Add shrimp and cook until no longer pink in color, which should take about 4 to 5 minutes.

2. Remove the shrimp from heat and let it cool. Add red pepper flakes and garlic to the skillet and sauté for a minute.

3. Remove the contents from heat and add wine to deglaze the skillet. Return the pan to heat, add in broth, and let it thicken.

4. Once thickened to preferred consistency, add in parsley. At this point, return the shrimp to the skillet and toss to coat.

5. Remove from the burner and serve it with vegetables.

25: Creamed Cabbage with Bacon

Serves 8

Ingredients

½ cup of cultured sour cream

1 ½ teaspoons of salt

1 head medium cabbage

4 tablespoons of coconut oil

5 medium-slices of bacon

Directions

1. In a large skillet, cook the bacon in medium heat for 5 minutes on each side.

2. When bacon is crispy, transfer to a paper towel to absorb excess fat and then set aside; let it cool and then crumble. Reserve about 3 tablespoons of bacon grease in the skillet.

3. Add coconut oil to the pan and heat over medium heat. Once the coconut oil melts, add salt and shredded cabbage.

4. Sauté for around 15 minutes while tossing 5-6 times. As soon as the ingredients have wilted and cooked through, add sour cream and stir.

5. To serve, top with crumbled bacon.

26: Roasted Vegetables

Serves 2-4

Ingredients

5 whole cloves of garlic

½ onion, sliced

1 yellow squash, sliced

1 zucchini, sliced

1 bunch of asparagus with the ends cut off

A sprinkle of pepper

A drizzle of olive oil

Directions

1. Preheat your oven to 450 degrees F.

2. Place the garlic cloves and vegetables on a lipped baking sheet and then drizzle some olive oil all over.

3. Add some pepper and stir.

4. Bake the vegetables for about 16 minutes, while stirring at 8 minutes interval.

5. As soon as the veggies slightly brown, remove from heat and serve.

27: Jicama Salad

Serves 6

Ingredients

1 lemon, juiced

½ bunch of cilantro, chopped

Ground black pepper

½ jalapeno pepper, diced

3 Thai Chile peppers, minced

4 radishes, thinly sliced

2 small sweet orange peppers, sliced

3 small sweet yellow peppers, sliced

½ hothouse cucumber, diced

1 large red bell pepper, chopped

2 navel oranges, cut into chunks

1 large jicama, peeled and julienned

Directions

1. In a large bowl, combine all the ingredients and mix well to incorporate.

2. Use plastic wrap to cover the bowl and chill for 30 minutes for flavors to blend.

3. Remove from refrigerator and serve.

28: Ethiopian Cabbage

Serves 1

Ingredients

5 red potatoes, peeled and cubed

½ head of cabbage, shredded

¼ teaspoon of ground turmeric

½ teaspoon of ground cumin

½ teaspoon of ground black pepper

1 teaspoon of sea salt

1 onion, thinly sliced

4 carrots, thinly sliced

½ cup of olive oil

Directions

1. Heat the olive oil in a skillet placed over medium high heat.

2. Cook the onion and carrots in olive oil for about 5 minutes.

3. Stir in cabbage, turmeric, cumin, salt, and pepper. Cook for 15-20 minutes.

4. Now add in potatoes, place the lid, and lower the heat to medium-low. Cook for about 20-30 minutes or until the potatoes are soft.

29: Roast Turkey

Makes 1 18lb. turkey

Ingredients

1 onion, quartered

1 lemon, quartered

½ teaspoon of pepper

½ teaspoon of salt

4 cloves of garlic, minced

1/3 cup of fresh thyme, finely chopped

½ cup of olive oil

18 pound fresh or frozen turkey, thawed

Directions

1. Preheat your oven to 325 degrees F; line a roasting pan with foil and set rack in pan.

2. Rinse the turkey inside and out using cold water. Put the meat on a rack, breast-side up. Pat dry using paper towels.

3. Mix together garlic, thyme, and pepper. Loosen the skin from the turkey meat and rub the garlic mixture under the skin and over the meat.

4. Put the onion pieces and lemon in the turkey cavity and tie together using heavy kitchen twine. Using a foil, cover the chicken loosely and bake for 3 hours.

5. Uncover and bake until the temperature reaches 165 degrees at the breast and thigh part of the turkey.

6. After around 1 hour of baking, remove from the oven and cover. Allow to cool for 10 minutes then carve it.

7. You can garnish with lemons, flat-leaf parsley, and fresh thyme or roasted Brussels sprouts.

30: Chicken Fajitas

Serves 4

Ingredients

¾ cup of Tessemae's Southwest Ranch

2 tablespoon of Tessemae's roasted Mediterranean Roasted Garlic Spread

3 bell peppers cut into strips

3 sliced yellow onions

3 free-range chicken breasts, cut into pieces

Organic butter-lettuce leaves

Tessemae's Hot Sauce

Directions

1. Combine the garlic spread, bell peppers, onions, Southwest Ranch Mix, and the chicken in a bowl.

2. Over medium heat, heat a wok or a large skillet, and then add the above mixture. Cook the contents until the veggies are soft and the chicken is ready.

3. Wrap the fajitas with butter lettuce and serve with hot sauce.

31: Grilled Salmon

Serves 4-6

Ingredients

¼ teaspoon of pepper, freshly ground

2 medium tomatoes, thinly sliced

¼ cup + 1/3 cup sliced fresh basil, divided

1 whole wild salmon fillet

1 tablespoon of extra-virgin olive oil

1 teaspoon of kosher salt, divided

2 cloves of garlic, minced

Directions

1. Preheat your grill to medium and on a cutting board; mash minced garlic and salt to get a paste.

2. Pour the paste into a small bowl and stir in oil. Prepare the salmon and remove any pin bones if desired.

3. Coat foil with cooking spray and then place the salmon on the foil; skin side facing down.

4. Now spread the garlic mixture on the fish and then sprinkle with about 1/3 cup of basil.

5. Overlap the tomato slices and sprinkle with pepper and ¼ teaspoon of salt.

6. Grill the fish (within the foil) until it flakes easily; about 10-12 minutes.

7. Use two large spatulas to slide the salmon onto a serving platter.

8. Serve the fish sprinkled with ¼ cup of basil.

32: Garlic Shrimp Noodle Bowls

Serves 2

Ingredients

10-20 peeled and deveined jumbo shrimps

2 tablespoons of olive oil

3, crushed cloves of garlic

For Cajun Seasoning

1 teaspoon of organic onion powder

1 teaspoon of paprika

Cayenne pepper to taste

Red pepper flakes to taste

½ teaspoon of salt (or to taste)

1 teaspoon of garlic granules

Optional

2 large spiralized zucchinis

1 tablespoon of olive oil

1 sliced red pepper

1 sliced onion

Directions

1. Use a spiralizer to spiralize your zucchini and set aside—you can also use a mandolin to spiralize

2. Place the shrimp in a bowl and season with the Cajun seasoning

3. Place a pan over medium-high heat and then heat the oil. Add the red pepper—if you are using—and onion, and sauté until the peppers and onions are soft but firm to the touch, it should take about 3-4 minutes.

4. Add the Cajun coated shrimp, cook for 3-5 minutes or until they turn opaque

5. Use a separate pan to heat the remaining olive oil and in this sauté the spiralized zucchinis for 1-3 minutes or until they are slightly soft but not soggy. Use a strainer to drain excess water.

6. Move the zucchini noodles to a bowl and use the Cajun shrimp and veggie mixtures to top. Taste for seasoning and if need be, add spices and salt as desired.

33: Kale Salad

Serves 2-3

Ingredients

½ red onion, very thinly sliced

2 bunches of kale

6 medjool dates, pitted

1/3 cup of whole hazelnuts

For the dressing

5 tablespoons of toasted hazelnut oil

Pinch of coarse salt

1 medjool date

4 tablespoons of orange juice, freshly squeezed

2 tablespoons of apple cider vinegar

Directions

1. Preheat your oven to 375 degrees F and then place hazelnuts on a baking dish. Roast the nuts for about 7-8 minutes, or until the skin begins to darken and split.

2. When done, transfer the nuts (while still hot) and steam for 15 minutes while wrapped in a kitchen towel.

3. Once cooled down, firmly squeeze and twist around to remove the skin all while still wrapped in the towel.

4. Put the hazelnuts in a food processor, and pulse them until fully mixed and finely chopped. Set them aside to top the salad.

5. Wash, dry, and chop the kale and then put in a large bowl. Slice the onion thinly and add into the bowl.

6. Prepare the dressing by combining all ingredients except the oil in ta blender. Puree the mixture to break down the dates and then drizzle the oil in a steady stream to emulsify the dressing.

7. Finally, toss the kale and onion mixture along with the orange-hazel nut dressing together.

8. Transfer to a platterl and sprinkle with the hazelnut and dates mixture. Serve!

34: Salmon with Broccoli

Serves 4

Ingredients

½ cup of water

2 tablespoons of pine nuts

3 tablespoons of raisins

1 small onion, diced

1 ½ tablespoons of extra-virgin olive oil, divided

2 heads of broccoli, trimmed

1 teaspoon salt, divided

1 teaspoon dried or 1 tablespoon fresh rosemary; chopped and divided

1 ¼ pounds of wild Alaskan salmon fillet cut into 4 pieces

Directions

1. Use ½-teaspoon of salt and half the rosemary to season the salmon and let it rest for about 20-60 minutes. Cut the broccoli into florets with 2-inch-long stalks.

2. Using a vegetable peeler, remove the tough covering of the stalk and cut the florets in half, lengthwise.

3. In a large and wide saucepan, heat a tablespoon of oil over medium heat. Add in onion and cook for about 3-4 minutes until translucent.

4. Add in the remaining rosemary, pine nuts and raisins, and toss to cover with oil. Continue to cook for 3-5 minutes, to have the pine nuts turn fragrant and start to brown.

5. Add in broccoli and season with ½-teaspoon of salt, tossing to combine. To this mixture, add in water and bring to boil and then reduce the heat to maintain a simmer.

6. Cook for about 8-10 minutes while stirring regularly. Cook until most of the water has evaporated.

7. Into a large non-stick skillet, heat ½ tablespoon of oil over medium heat. Add in the salmon, the skinned side facing up, and cook for 3-5 minutes, until golden brown.

8. Turn it over, remove pan from the heat, and allow it to stand until cooked through; for an additional 3-5 minutes.

9. When done, divide broccoli into 4 plates and top with the salmon, pine nuts, raisins and the remaining liquid from the pan.

35: Chicken Ranch Taco Salad

Serves 2

Ingredients

½ pound of leftover, cooked and chopped chicken

1½ tablespoons of Paleo taco seasoning (recipe included below)

1 teaspoon of coconut oil

¼ cup of water

Lettuce, shredded

Toppings of choice such as red onion, sliced olives, bell peppers, tomatoes, hot sauce, etc.)

Raw ranch dressing

Crushed sweet potato chips (as a non-optional topping)

For Taco Seasoning

To make the taco seasoning, mix 4 tablespoons of chili powder, 1 teaspoon of garlic, 1 teaspoon of onion powder, 1 teaspoon of oregano, 2 teaspoons of paprika, 2 teaspoons of cumin, 4 teaspoons of sea salt, and ¼ teaspoon of red pepper flakes.

Directions

1.. Heat oil in a skillet, add in the chicken, and fry for a minute to give the chicken flavor. After the minute, add in the water and let the chicken simmer until all the water evaporates.

2. Meanwhile, prepare your toppings by shredding, chopping and dicing what needs shredding, chopping, or dicing.

4. Assemble everything and serve.

36: Garlic Chicken

Serves: 4-6

Ingredients

¼ teaspoon of pepper

½ teaspoon of salt

1 ½ teaspoon of crushed basil

1 ½ pounds of cherry tomatoes

2 pounds chicken cutlets

1 tablespoon of chopped garlic- about 4 cloves

¾ cup of diced red onion

2 tablespoon of olive oil

Directions

1. Heat oil in a large skillet over medium heat, and then add in onion and garlic. Cook for about 5 minutes. Regularly mix the ingredients using a spatula.

2. Add in the chicken to the pan, and cook for about 3-4 minutes on each side to brown. Thicker chicken breasts may take longer; about 6-8 minutes.

3. Chop the cherry tomatoes in a blender or food processor. Add to the pan with the chicken and combine.

4. Add in pepper, salt and basil, and bring to a boil. Let simmer for about 25 minutes before serving.

37: Stuffed Peppers

Serves 4

Ingredients

¼ cup of beef stock

Salt and pepper to taste

¼ cup of homemade Italian seasoning blend

6 ounces of tomato paste

4 cloves of garlic, minced

1 carrot, diced

1 onion, diced

½ head of cauliflower

1 pound of ground meat

4 bell peppers

Directions

1. Pulse garlic, carrots, onion, and cauliflower in a food processor, until fine.

2. Cut off the top of peppers and keep them intact. Remove the seeds.

3. Combine pepper, salt, seasonings, tomato paste, meat and vegetables in a mixing bowl, and then spoon this mixture into the peppers. Ensure you level the peppers off at the top and position them in the slow cooker.

4. Place the tops of the peppers onto the peppers. Pour the liquid in the bottom of the slow cooker, and then cook the mixture on low for about 6-8 hours. Serve.

38: Mayo Steak Salad

Serves 4

Ingredients

2 tablespoon of extra virgin olive oil, divided

¼ cup of cilantro

½ jicama

1 whole avocado, diced

2 medium tomatoes (raw), diced

8 oz. fresh spinach

8 oz. steak

For Dressing

Sea salt and pepper

1 tablespoon of olive oil

Juice of 3 to 4 limes

Directions

1. Season the steak with salt and pepper. Add olive oil to a cast iron skillet, over medium-high heat and fry the steak for around 4 minutes, flip, and cook the other side for 3-4 minutes.

3. Remove the steak from heat and let it cool down for 10 minutes. Then slice it thinly.

4. Meanwhile, toss the veggies in a large bowl and start to make the dressing. Just juice the limes in a bowl and whisk in olive oil. You can season with pepper and salt to taste.

5. To serve, top the salad with the steak, and season with the dressing.

39: Paleo Coconut Soup

Serves 4-6

Ingredients

1 teaspoon of Sriracha

1 tablespoon of fish sauce

2 tablespoons of lime juice

2 oz. of sliced mushrooms

1 teaspoon of ginger root

1 pound of shrimp

2 cups of chicken broth

14 ounces of organic coconut milk

Directions

1. Peel and devein the shrimp, or if using chicken clean it and cut into small chunks.

2. Mix ginger, chicken stock and coconut milk in a pot placed over medium heat and then bring the mixture to a boil. Lower the heat and allow it to simmer.

3. Now add in Sriracha, fish sauce, lime juice, mushrooms and the chicken or shrimp and simmer

until the meat cooks through. The chicken should take 10 minutes and the shrimp less than 5 minutes.

4. Spoon out the ginger rounds and discard, and garnish with fresh chopped cilantro.

40: Chinese Chicken Salad

Serves: 4

Ingredients

2 tablespoons of rice vinegar

1 tablespoon of peanut oil

1 tablespoon of sesame seeds

1 tablespoon of hoisin sauce

4 cups of torn romaine lettuce

2 cups of cooked chicken, chopped

3½ ounces of Enoki mushrooms

1 can sliced water chestnuts, drained

3 scallions, sliced into thin round

1 rib celery, finely chipped

1 teaspoon of sesame oil

1 teaspoon of mustard powder

½ teaspoon of Sriracha sauce, optional

Directions

1. In a large salad bowl, combine celery, scallions, water chestnuts, mushrooms, chicken, and lettuce.

2. In a separate bowl, whisk together Sriracha sauce, mustard powder, sesame oil, hoisin sauce, sesame seeds, peanut oil, and vinegar.

3. Pour this sauce over the vegetables and chicken and then toss to mix. Serve

41: Sardine Stuffed Avocado

Serves 1-2

Ingredients

¼ teaspoon of Himalayan salt

1 teaspoon of turmeric root, freshly ground

1 tablespoon of fresh lemon juice

1 medium spring onion or a bunch of chives

1 tablespoon of mayonnaise

1 tin of sardines, drained

1 large avocado

Directions

1. Cut the avocado in half and remove the seed. Drain the sardines and put them in a bowl.

2. Scoop the flesh from the avocado half but leave ½-1 inch of avocado flesh. Then add in finely sliced spring onions and ground turmeric root. Follow with mayonnaise and mix well.

3. Add in the scooped avocado flesh, mash into your preferred smoothness, and squeeze in fresh lemon juice and salt.

4. To serve, scoop the avocado mixture into each avocado half.

42: Quinoa Salad with Cashews

Serves 4

Ingredients

3 cups Romaine lettuce, chopped

1 cup cashews, coarsely chopped

1 avocado, chopped or thinly sliced

½-inch-piece ginger, finely chopped

Black pepper, freshly ground

1 teaspoon of sea salt, to taste

¼ cup of mint, finely chopped

1 large mango, chopped

1 tablespoon of extra-virgin olive oil

2 tablespoons of honey

Juice of 1 lime

1 cup apple or carrot, finely chopped

½ red onion, finely chopped

1 cup dried quinoa, rinsed well

Directions

1. To cook the quinoa, bring 2 cups of water to a boil in a saucepan, and then add quinoa. Cover and simmer for around 15-20 minutes. Once cooked through, set aside and let it cool.

2. Toss the apple or carrot with chopped onions in a large bowl. In a separate bowl, whisk together olive oil, honey and lime juice, and add the mixture to the bowl.

3. Add in cooked quinoa and mango and toss to mix. Add in ginger, cilantro, mint, pepper, and salt.

4. Garnish with cashews and sliced avocado. To serve, scoop the mixture over the greens.

43: Stir-Fry Vegetables

Serves 4

Ingredients

1 tablespoon of Oriental seasoning

1 cup of yellow squash, thinly sliced

1 cup of zucchini, thinly sliced

½ cup of cauliflower, chopped

3 carrots, peeled and sliced

1 teaspoon of sea salt

1 bell pepper, sliced

½ cup of broccoli, chopped

3 celery stalks, thinly sliced

1 red onion, sliced

Directions

1. First, stir-fry all the veggies in olive oil until tender and then add salt and other seasonings.

2. Serve, preferably over cauliflower 'rice'.

44: Paleo Tacos

Serves 4-5

Ingredients

1 avocado, sliced

½ cup of cilantro, chopped

½ zucchini, shredded

½ purple onion, diced

1 large tomato, seeded and diced

3 tablespoons of olive oil

1 serrano pepper, sliced

1 garlic clove, minced

1/8 teaspoon of cayenne pepper

½ teaspoon of chili powder

2 teaspoons of coriander

2 teaspoons of cumin

2 cups of raw walnuts

1 head of iceberg lettuce

Nutritional yeast to taste

Salt and pepper to taste

Directions

1. Rinse the lettuce, drain and set aside. Place the walnuts in a food processor, and pulse until fully ground.

2. Add in Serrano pepper, garlic, cayenne pepper, chili powder, coriander, cumin and olive oil, and continue to pulse to incorporate the mixture.

3. Chop the butt of the iceberg lettuce, and slice the head into two. To reveal the cups, gently pull apart the layers.

4. Spoon the walnut mixture into the cups, and top with diced tomatoes, chopped cilantro, shredded zucchini, and onion.

5. Slide in a few avocado slices and season with salt and pepper. Top with nutritional yeast and serve.

45: Steak and Sriracha Lettuce Wraps

Yields 6 lettuce wraps

Ingredients

1 bell pepper, diced

1 pound of fajita strips, diced into ½" bite sizes

2 tablespoons of Sriracha

Enough sesame oil for drizzling

3 cloves of garlic, diced

Enough green onions for garnishing

A handful of pea shoots

1 large onion, diced

2 teaspoons of coconut aminos (or soy sauce)

Large lettuce leaves (preferably iceberg romaine)

Directions

1. Place a pan over medium-high heat and let it heat up before adding in oil. Heat the oil for 1 minute or so or until it's shimmery.

2. Add the fajita meat to the pan and cook on high heat for 3 minutes remembering to toss occasionally.

3. Add in the onions and peppers. Continue cooking on high while still tossing occasionally; cook for 5 minutes or until browned.

4. Add in the garlic, sesame oil, Sriracha, the coconut aminos, and the pea shoots.

5. When the veggies and steak coat well and have absorbed the sauce, remove from heat, let it cool for a while, and then spoon the mixture into lettuce cups. Top with the diced green onions and then serve warm.

Dinner Recipes

46: Pork Chops with Avocado Salad

Serves 4

Ingredients

½ teaspoon of Dijon mustard (Paleo friendly)

1 tablespoon of red wine vinegar

3 tablespoons of extra-virgin olive oil

1 tablespoon of walnuts, toasted and chopped

¼ small red onion, thinly sliced

1 bunch of watercress or arugula

1 avocado, cut into medium chunks

Grape seed or olive oil

4 bone-in pork chops, trimmed of fat

Kosher salt and pepper

¼ teaspoon of garlic powder

1/8 teaspoon of cayenne

1 teaspoon of coriander

1 tablespoon of organic honey

1 teaspoon of coffee, finely ground

Directions

1. Combine coffee, honey coriander, cayenne, garlic, and pepper along with salt to taste.

2. Rub the meat with canola or grape-seed oil and then with the spice blend.

3. Grill on medium heat until done or for about 5 to 7 minutes. The temperature near the center of the meat should be around 155 degrees F.

4. Mix walnuts, onion, watercress, and avocadoes in a bowl.

5. In a small bowl, whisk together olive oil, mustard, vinegar, and salt. Toss the spices with the vegetables.

47: Chicken Thighs with Butternut Squash

Serves: 4-6

Ingredients

Freshly chopped sage

½ pound of organic, nitrate free bacon

Extra olive or coconut oil for frying

2-3 cups of cubed butternut squash

Salt and pepper to taste (as you season the meal, keep in mind the salty nature of the bacon, and therefore, use the salt sparingly)

6 chicken thighs, boneless and skinless

Directions

1. Preheat your oven to 425 degrees F.

2. In a large pan placed over medium-high heat, fry the bacon until crispy. Set aside and let cool. After the bacon cools, crumble.

3. Use the same skillet (and the bacon grease) to sauté the butternut squash until soft; seasoning accordingly using salt and pepper—keeping in mind the salty nature of the bacon grease—and once soft, transfer to a plate.

4. Add coconut oil to the same skillet (only if the butternuts have soaked up most if not all the bacon grease). Add in the chicken thighs with the top down and cook for 10 minutes—you can use the salt and pepper to season as desired.

5. Turn the thighs and immediately after, return the squash to the skillet and arrange it all around the thighs.

6. Turn off the heat and remove the skillet from the stovetop. Transfer it to the preheated oven and let the meal bake for 12-15 minutes or until the chicken cooks through.

7. Remove from the oven and top the meal with the crumbled bacon and fresh sage, serve.

48: Quinoa with Tomato Sauce

Serves 2

Ingredients

2 tablespoons of extra-virgin olive oil, cold-pressed

1 pinch of cayenne pepper

½ teaspoon of sea salt

3 tablespoons of fresh basil

1 teaspoon of vegetable stock, yeast-free

1 ounce of pine nuts

1 clove of garlic

1 medium-sized onion

8 ounces of artichoke hearts, fresh or frozen

5 ounces of tomatoes

7 ounces of quinoa

Directions

1. Cook the artichoke until tender, or alternatively, use frozen artichoke hearts.

2. Cook the quinoa according to its package directions. As it cooks, cut the tomatoes into cubes, and then chop the basil, garlic, and onion into pieces.

3. In a pan, heat 2 tablespoons of olive oil and stir-fry onions, pine nuts, and garlic for a few minutes. Then add in the cooked artichoke hearts and tomatoes and cook for 2 minutes.

4. Dissolve the vegetable stock in ½ cup of water, in a pan. Let it simmer for 2 minutes on low heat as you stir regularly.

5. At the end, add in basil and season with salt and cayenne pepper. To serve, pour the sauce over the quinoa.

49: White Turkey Chili

Serves: 4-6

Ingredients

½ teaspoon of onion powder

½ teaspoon of garlic powder

2 teaspoons of cumin

2 ½ teaspoons of Ancho chili powder

1 onion

1 Poblano pepper

1 tablespoon of olive oil

2 cups of cooked turkey

4 cups of turkey broth

1 cup of water

1 head of cauliflower

Garnish:

Chopped tomatoes

Avocado

Cilantro

Directions

1. Add a cup of water into a large stockpot and then set the heat to high.

2. Chop the cauliflower roughly and put it into the stockpot. Once the water begins to boil lower the heat to medium.

3. Cook covered for 10-12 minutes to soften the cauliflower as you occasionally check if you need more water. Meanwhile, add olive oil to a skillet and set the heat to medium.

4. Coarsely chop the onions and add to the olive oil to cook for around 3-5 minutes.

5. Prepare the Poblano pepper by chopping and removing the seeds, and then dice. Add it to the onions and then cook for 3-4 more minutes.

6. Chop the already cooked turkey.

7. Drain the cauliflower and add it and the broth into a blender or immersion blender and process until smooth. Set aside

8. Add in the turkey, onions, peppers and spices, to the poblano pepper mixture and cook for 5-10 minutes. Serve and enjoy.

50: Zucchini Pasta and Chicken Pesto

Serves 4

Ingredients

4 oz. of red sauce (tomato sauce)

4 tablespoons of basil pesto

4 zucchini

4 chicken breasts

Fresh pepper to taste

Himalayan sea salt

For Basil Pesto

Fresh pepper to taste

Himalayan sea salt

3 cloves garlic

¼ cup of pine nuts

½ cup of extra virgin olive oil

3 bunches of basil

Red Sauce

Fresh pepper to taste

Himalayan sea salt

1 oz. of coconut oil

1 teaspoon of basil, dried

1 teaspoon of thyme, dried

1 teaspoon of oregano, dried

4 garlic cloves, minced

4 onions, minced

4-28oz. cans of plum tomatoes

Directions

1. First, season the chicken with salt and pepper and then grill over medium heat. Meanwhile, simmer water in a pot to steam the zucchini.

2. Warm up the red sauce and maintain it at a low simmer, and slice the zucchini lengthwise to obtain thin strips.

3. Steam the zucchini just about 3 minutes before your chicken cooks through.

4. Spoon the red sauce onto a plate, and mix zucchini with the pesto; then plate onto the red sauce.

5. Slice the chicken, put it over the noodles, and then serve. Start making the basil pesto now.

6. In a food processor, add garlic and basil leaves. Mix and add olive oil followed by pine nuts.

7. Taste and season with salt and pepper as desired. To make the red sauce, follow the following steps.

Red Sauce

1. In a large pot placed over low heat, sauté the onions in oil until they are translucent.

2. Add in garlic and herbs, and continue to cook for a few minutes. Remove from heat.

3. Add tomatoes and then use an emulsion blender to puree.

4. Simmer the mixture until it reduces to about 2/3rd, and then add in salt and pepper to taste.

5. Serve immediately or alternatively cool and freeze.

51: Arugula Salad with Pan Seared Fish

Serves: 2

Ingredients

For Salad

1 tablespoon of flax seeds

1 ruby red grapefruit or orange, chilled

1 large avocado

1 bunch of arugula or baby arugula

For Dressing

¼ teaspoon of black pepper

1 tablespoon of miso

2 tablespoons of honey

¼ tablespoon of olive oil

½ cup of apple cider vinegar

The Fish

1 egg

2 filets of tilapia (omit the flour if using Salmon)

¼ teaspoon of salt

1 tablespoon of Cajun seasoning

½ cup almond flour

Directions

1. Put Cajun seasoning and almond flour on a plate and mix well.

2. Crack the egg into a bowl, and beat and then dredge the fish filet through the egg. Use the flour and Cajun seasoning mixture to cover both sides. Shake off the excess and then set aside.

3. Prepare a large bowl, and then wash and spin-dry the arugula. Put it into the bowl.

4. Place the dressing ingredients into a jar, seal and shake to combine. Pour ¼ cup of the arugula and flax seeds then toss to cover. Put the arugula into a serving plate.

5. Cut the grape fruit into sections or wheels, and the avocado into slices. Alternately, place the slices in a circle on top of the arugula and add a little more dressing.

6. On high, heat 1-2 tablespoons of olive oil in a stainless steel pan. Wait until the oil starts smoking and then add filet in the pan. Cook until it lifts easily from the pan.

7. Flip the filet over and cook for 2 additional minutes while uncovered.

8. Pour about ¼ cup of water in a pan and then steam to cook the fish through. Then put the fish onto the salad and enjoy.

52: Coconut Shrimp "Pasta"

Serves 2

Ingredients

2 large zucchinis, peel on, stringed

¼ teaspoon of garam masala

Juice of 1 lime

¼ cup of fresh cilantro, chopped

½ cup of coconut cream

300g cooked shrimp

1 small onion, very finely chopped

225g of mushrooms, sliced

½ teaspoon of black pepper, freshly cracked

½ teaspoon of fine sea salt or Himalayan

1 cup of pure coconut water

¾ cup of water

600g of cauliflower, roughly chopped

Directions

1. In a medium saucepan, add in pure coconut water, water, and cauliflower and bring to a boil. Reduce the heat to low and cook covered for about 5-7 minutes to soften the cauliflower fully.

2. In a large skillet, cook the mushrooms until golden, then add in pepper, salt and onions, and continue to cook until soft and fragrant.

3. Then in a blender, ladle the cauliflower mixture and process on high speed to achieve a smooth and silky consistency.

4. Now pour the cauliflower mixture over the onions and mushrooms and add in Garam masala, lime juice, coconut cream, and cooked shrimp.

5. Over low-medium heat, bring the mixture to a simmer to warm the shrimp and then stir in fresh cilantro.

6. To serve, divide the stringed zucchini between 2 plates and ladle shrimp sauce over it

53: Spice-Rubbed Bison Tenderloin

Serves: 4

Ingredients

4 6-ounce bison or beef tenderloin filets

½ teaspoon of gray sea salt or pink rock salt

1 teaspoon of minced fresh ginger root

½ teaspoon of allspice

2 teaspoons of cumin seeds, dry-toasted and ground

2 teaspoons of coriander seeds, ground

1 teaspoon of cinnamon

2 tablespoons of minced garlic

2 sprigs of fresh rosemary

Directions

1. Mix the ginger root, spices, garlic, and rosemary in a small bowl and set aside.

2. Put the bison or beef on a 12 x 12 inch glass-baking dish, and then use the spice mix to coat both sides.

3. Now preheat the broiler on low and then put the fillets under it, around 6 inches from heat. Use medium low heat if using a grill pan on a stove.

4. Drizzle the meat with broth or filtered water to keep it moist. This also ensures your spices do not catch fire.

5. Grill or broil for around 4 to 6 minutes until done, while checking the meat not to overcook it.

6. As soon as it is done, remove from the grill or oven and let it cool. Serve and enjoy.

54: Chicken Puttanesca with Artichokes

Serves 4

Ingredients

2 tablespoons of fresh parsley, chopped

¼ cup of fresh basil, chopped

1 tablespoon of capers, chopped

1/4 cup kalamata olives, chopped

1 14.5 oz. can of salt-free artichoke hearts, halved

1 14.5 oz. can of tomatoes, no-salt-added

1 tablespoon of anchovy paste

1 tablespoon red pepper, crushed

½ tablespoon of thyme, dried

3 cloves garlic, minced

1 yellow bell pepper, diced

¼ cup of dry white wine

1 large yellow onion, diced

Salt and pepper

2 8-oz boneless, skinless chicken breasts, halved

1 tablespoon olive oil, divided

Directions

1. Heat a tablespoon of oil in a large pan, over medium heat.

2. Season the meat with a little salt and pepper and then cook until cooked through for about 5-7 minutes. Once the chicken breast browns, remove from heat and transfer onto a plate.

3. Add the remaining oil to the pan and then lower the heat to medium. Add onions and sauté for around 2 minutes and then add in bell pepper. In case the brown onion bits appear to burn, deglaze with the dry white wine.

4. As soon as the sautéed onions turn transparent and soft, add in anchovy paste, red peeper, dried thyme, and garlic. Cook the mixture for a minute as you stir, or until fragrant.

5. Now add in the capers, olives, tomatoes and the remaining wine, and then allow the mixture to simmer.

6. Put the chicken back in the pan and add in the sauce and chicken juices. Cover and simmer the mixture for about 20 minutes.

7. Once the sauce slightly reduces and the chicken cooks through, stir in the fresh herbs and adjust the seasoning based on your preferred taste.

55: Crockpot Beef Roast and Veggies

Servings: 6-8

Ingredients

3 cloves of garlic, minced

1 onion, chopped

6 carrots, chopped

6 celery stalks, chopped

2 sweet potato, cut into cubes

2 cups of bone broth beef or chicken stock

4 pounds of beef roast

1 tablespoon of paprika

1 tablespoon of onion powder

1 tablespoon of garlic powder

1 tablespoon of pepper

1 tablespoon salt

Directions

1. Mix all the seasonings in a small bowl to create a spice rub.

2. Massage the spice rub all over the beef. You can also refrigerate the beef for at least 3 hours to let the rub set in.

3. Put the beef into the slow cooker and pour in the broth.

4. Add the remaining ingredients and cook on low for about 8 hours.

5. Once done, remove the beef from the slow cooker and put it onto a cutting board.

7. Use tongs or two forks to shred it and then serve with the veggies.

56: Almond Salmon with Roasted Fennel

Serves 2

Ingredients

2 tablespoons of shaved almonds

2 teaspoons of local honey, organic

2 8oz. wild salmon filets

Lemon juice

Sea salt

Olive oil

1 fennel bulb

Roasted Fennel

Directions

1. Preheat your oven to around 400 degrees F.

2. Cut the stems from the fennel, which you can preserve for garnish or soups if desired, chop the white bulb into chunks, and then drizzle with olive oil, pepper, and salt.

3. Roast the fennel uncovered for around 30 minutes, and then spread the honey on salmon filets. Top with shaved almonds.

4. Place the salmon onto a roasting or baking pan with the skin side facing down. After the fennel has been in the oven for 30 minutes, pop in the salmon.

5. Bake both until the fish cooks through and almonds brown, in around 12 minutes.

57: Pork and Sweet Potato Skillet

Serves 4

Ingredients

2 teaspoons of white wine vinegar

1 tablespoons of fresh rosemary, chopped

2 tablespoon of chopped, fresh thyme

2 large, bone-in pork chops

1 ½ pound of red potatoes cut into bite-size pieces

½ large red onion, chopped

4 cloves of garlic, minced

2 tablespoons of olive oil

Salt & Pepper to taste

Directions

1. Preheat your oven to 350 degrees F as you warm some oil in a large heatproof skillet.

2. Add in onion and garlic and cook until the onions turn translucent. Stir in the chopped potatoes and continue cooking for 10 minutes. Your potatoes should just turn slightly soft.

3. Add in pork chops, rosemary, and thyme together with the white wine vinegar. Brown your chops on each side.

4. Move the skillet into the preheated oven and cook for 30-40 minutes.

5. Once the potatoes cook through and meat reaches 165 degrees F, serve. Season the potato, pork and veggies dish with salt and pepper

58: Root Vegetable Tagine

Serves 6

Ingredients

¼ cup of cilantro leaves roughly chopped

2 tablespoons of lemon juice

2 cups of kale leaves, roughly chopped

1 quart of vegetable stock

2 medium diced carrots or 2 bunches of baby carrots, peeled

2 medium purple potatoes, peeled and diced

2 medium sweet potatoes, peeled and diced

3 tablespoons of tomato paste

¼ teaspoon of cayenne pepper

½ teaspoon of ground cinnamon

1 teaspoon of sea salt

½ teaspoon of ground ginger

1 teaspoon of ground cumin

2 large cloves of garlic, minced

1 medium parsnip, peeled and diced

1 large sweet onion, diced

2 tablespoons of olive or coconut oil

Slivered almonds, toasted

Directions

1. Heat the oil in a large stockpot. Over medium heat, sauté the onion for 5 minutes or until soft, and then add in parsnip.

2. Cook until golden brown, or for 3 minutes. Stir in tomato paste, cayenne, salt, cinnamon, ginger, ground cumin, and garlic.

3. Cook for 2 minutes or until very fragrant then fold in carrots, purple potatoes, and sweet potatoes.

4. Add vegetable stock and bring to a boil, then lower the heat to medium-low. Simmer uncovered for around 20 minutes or until veggies are tender, while stirring after a few minutes.

5. Stir in lemon juice and kale and simmer until the leaves are vibrant and slightly wilted, in about 2 minutes.

6. Garnish the dish with nuts and cilantro if you like. Serve over quinoa.

59: Whole Baked Trout with Herb Salsa and Lemon

Serves 4

Ingredients

2, 1lb. whole trout fish

For the salsa

¼ teaspoon of black pepper

Fresh parsley, a handful

1 peeled garlic clove

½ cup of olive oil

1 medium-sized red onion, peeled and roughly diced

2 teaspoons of sea salt

Zest of 1 lemon

Juice of ½ lemon with the remaining half sliced into rounds to put atop the fish

Fresh basil leaves, a handful

Mint leaves

Directions

1. Preheat your oven to 200 degrees F.

2. In the meantime, use a blender or food processor to mix and process the salsa ingredients until you get a salsa like consistency.

3. Place the fish in a large roasting tray, use the herb marinade to cover both sides of the fish and the cavity—as further down as you can go—place lemon slices on top of the fish and bake in the preheated oven for 20-25 minutes on the middle shelve.

4. Remove carefully to a platter or if you fear the fish shall break apart as you do so, serve it in the roasting tray.

60: Chicken Butternut Squash Hazelnut Mash

Serves 2

Ingredients

¼ cup of coconut milk

50g of hazelnuts, crushed

6 cups of baby spinach leaves, fresh and chopped

Juice of one orange

Freshly cracked pepper, few grinds

Himalayan or fine sea salt

2-200g chicken breasts, boneless and skinless

½ teaspoon of chai spice

1-800g butternut squash, seeds removed, halved

Directions

1. Preheat the oven to 350 degrees F. Sprinkle a little salt and pepper onto the butternut squash halves.

2. In a large and shallow baking pan, put the butternut squash halves face down.

3. Put the chicken breasts and the squash in the same large pan. Sprinkle them with salt and pepper and

then squeeze some orange juice over your chicken. Place the empty orange shells in the pan and then cover using foil.

4. Bake the mixture in the oven for about 30-35 minutes. When done, the squash should look nice and soft. Now take away the foil and let it cool down.

5. Add spinach to a large and non-stick skillet and cook for about 2-3 minutes, or until wilted. You can also wilt the spinach by putting it into the microwave for 1-2 minutes.

6. Toast the hazelnuts in a small and dry pan placed over medium heat.

7. In a large bowl, shred the chicken into bite sizes. Use a spoon to scoop the flesh out of a squash, and then add in the chicken.

8. Add in chai spice, coconut cream, hazel nuts, and spinach and mix completely.

9. Sub-divide the contents among 2 heat-safe dishes and then broil until brown.

10. Garnish with coconut cream or more crushed hazelnuts.

61: Kelp Noodles with Avocado Pesto

Serves 4

Ingredients

1 package of kelp noodles

1-2 cloves garlic

1 teaspoon of salt

¼ cup of fresh basil

1 cup of fresh baby spinach leaves

½ cup of extra virgin olive oil

1 hass avocado

Directions

1. First rinse the noodles, and then soak in water for 30 to 45 minutes.

2. Carefully break them apart from the clump.

3. Meanwhile, mix other ingredients in a food processor or blender and blitz until smooth. You can leave some bits of leaves showing if you like it!

4. At this point, remove the soaked noodles from water, drain and add ¼ cup of pesto per bag of kelp noodles.

5. Mix the noodles and pesto until well incorporated, and then top with other Paleo ingredients.

62: Poached Eggs with Curried Potatoes

Serves: 4

Ingredients

½ bunch of fresh cilantro

4 large eggs

1 15 oz. can of tomato sauce

2 tablespoons of curry powder

1 tablespoon of olive oil

2 cloves garlic

1 inch of fresh ginger

2 russet potatoes

Directions

1. Cut the potatoes into ¾-inch cubes then put the cubes in a pot. Add water, put on the lid, and bring the potatoes to a boil over high heat.

2. Boil the cubed potatoes until tender when pierced with a fork, or around 5-6 minutes. Drain and put them in a colander.

3. Meanwhile, start to prepare the sauce. Using the side of a spoon or vegetable peeler, peel the skin off

the ginger and then use a small holed cheese grater to grate about 1 inch of ginger.

4. Mince the garlic then put in a large deep skillet. Add in olive oil and garlic then sauté over medium low heat until soft and fragrant, in about 1-2 minutes.

5. To the skillet, add curry powder and sauté for a minute to toast the spices. Then add in tomato sauce and stir to blend.

6. Raise the heat to medium for the sauce to heat through. Taste and adjust the salt as needed.

7. Add the drained potatoes and stir to coat with the sauce. If need be, add a few tablespoons of water.

8. At this point, make 4 dips or wells in the potato mixture and crack the egg into each. Put on the lid and simmer for around 6-10 minutes or until cooked through.

9. Top the meal with chopped fresh cilantro.

63: Sweet Potato Turkey Casserole with Tomato & Eggplant

Serves 6

Ingredients

For the casserole

1 tablespoon of minced garlic

1 lb. of extra lean ground turkey

8 oz. of tomato paste

¼ teaspoon of chili powder

¼ cup of finely chopped onion

1/8 teaspoon of cardamom

1 medium-sized, peeled and spiralized sweet potato

¼ teaspoon of cumin

1 medium-sized eggplant cut into ½ inch pieces (you can also use a zucchini)

½ teaspoon of tarragon and more for topping

15 oz. petite-diced tomatoes with the liquid drained

1/8 teaspoon of oregano

½ teaspoon of pepper and salt each

For the sauce

1 tablespoon of coconut flour

1 tablespoon of almond flour

1 ½ tablespoon of olive oil, extra virgin

1 cup of almond milk, unsweetened (you can also use any other Paleo friendly milk substitute)

Directions

1. Preheat your oven to 350 F. Spray nonstick cooking spray into an 8X8 inch, squared casserole dish

2. Place a large pan over medium-high heat and then cook the ground beef, with the garlic and onion added to it, until browned; as the meat browns, break it up. Stir in the tomatoes and the tomato paste, and combine them with the meat. Add in the sweat potatoes and cook until they soften slightly.

3. In a bowl, mix all the seasonings, place the chopped eggplant into the bowl, and toss to combine. Remove the eggplant from the spice mix and layer them at the bottom of the casserole dish. Top with the sweet potato and turkey mixture and bake for 15 minutes.

4. In the meantime, prepare the sauce by boiling a small pot of water. To this, add in olive oil and the almond and coconut flours and boil while stirring in 1-

minute intervals until the mixture thickens. After, reduce the heat to medium-high and slowly add in the almond milk as you continue stirring. Stir until the sauce reduces by half, which should take about 10 minutes.

5. Once the 15 minutes are up, remove the casserole from the oven and use the sauce in the small pot to top. Return the casserole to the oven and bake for 40-45 minutes or until the casserole browns to a desired color. Remove from the oven, top with tarragon, slice into 6 pieces, and serve hot.

64: Paleo Basil & Tomato Chicken

Serves: 4

Ingredients

1 cup of cherry tomatoes, sliced in half

½ teaspoon of arrowroot powder

1 pound of chicken thighs or breasts, boneless and skinless

½ cup of canned coconut milk

½ yellow onion

1/3 cup of cold water

1 batch of nut-free, dairy-free pesto—the recipe is below

1 teaspoon of coconut oil

For the Nut-Free, Dairy-Free Pesto

3 cloves of garlic

1 tablespoon of avocado oil

2 tablespoons of sunflower seeds

Salt and pepper

2/3 oz. of fresh basil

1 tablespoon of nutritional yeast

Directions

1. Prepare the pesto by placing the garlic in a food processor and pulsing it into a fine mince. Add the sunflower seeds and pulse a few times. Add the nutritional yeast, a bit of salt, and a dash of pepper. Add in the avocado oil and basil, and then pulse the mixture until the basil is a fine mince. Set aside.

2. Place a large skillet over medium-high heat and to this, add the coconut oil and heat it until it sizzles. As the oil heats, cut the onion into strips and once done, add it to the pan and cook until the onions turn translucent.

3. When the onions are translucent, place the chicken into the pan and sear/cook each side for 12-13 minutes or until the chicken cooks through with the juices in the middle running clear.

4. Transfer the water into a small bowl and then whisk in the arrowroot. Add in coconut milk, and whisk in the pesto. Pour this mixture into the skillet with the chicken and bring the skillet to a gentle simmer.

5. Add in the sliced cherry tomatoes and let simmer for 1-2 minutes or until the tomatoes are warm. Serve over spiralized sweet potatoes.

65: Grilled Shrimp Scampi

Serves 6

Ingredients

1 ½ pounds of medium shrimp, peeled and deveined

Red pepper flakes, crushed, to taste

Black pepper, ground, to taste

1 tablespoon of minced garlic

3 tablespoons of fresh parsley, chopped

¼ cup lemon juice

¼ cup of olive oil

Directions

1. Stir together black pepper, garlic, parsley, lemon juice, and olive oil in a large non-reactive bowl.

2. Add some crushed red pepper to season and then add in the shrimp, tossing to coat. Marinate the mixture in the fridge for 30 minutes.

3. Preheat your grill under high heat and thread the shrimp onto your skewers. Pierce once near the tail of the shrimp and once again near the head. Discard the marinade.

3. Slightly oil the grill grate and then grill the chicken for around 3 minutes on each side or until it is opaque.

66: Shepherd's Pie with Cauliflower Topping

Serves 4-6

Ingredients

1 pound of ground beef or lamp

2 tablespoons of parsley, chopped

1 small red onion, diced

1 head of cauliflower chopped into florets

2 diced carrots

Salt and pepper to taste

2 tablespoons coconut oil (plus some additional 2 tablespoons for greasing)

1 tablespoon of homemade, Paleo-friendly tomato paste of ketchup

¼-½ cup of homemade beef broth

2 diced celery ribs

2 minced garlic cloves

Directions

1. Preheat your oven to 400 degrees F. Grease a 2X3 casserole dish and set it aside.

2. Steam or boil the cauliflower in a large pot, until tender.

3. In a large saucepan or large skillet placed over medium-high heat, heat 2 tablespoons of your fat. Add in the onion, celery, carrot and garlic and cook for 5 minutes or until they start to soften.

4. Add in the ground meat and cook until browned making sure to add the beef broth as needed to keep the mixture wet. Add the tomato paste or ketchup (this ingredient is optional and if you do not have a Paleo-friendly option, you can omit), parsley, and season with salt and pepper to taste. Let the mix simmer. In the meantime, prepare the cauliflower topping.

5. Drain the cooked cauliflower then puree until smooth using an emulsion blender (you can also mash). Add 2 tablespoons of fat and season to taste.

6. Assemble the meal by spreading the meat mixture on the bottom of the dish and then using a spoon to smooth the cauliflower topping over it. Bake for 30 minutes or until the top turns brown and bubbly, take out from the oven, let cool for a while, and serve warm

67: Beef with Brussels Sprouts

Serves 6

Ingredients

Leaves from 2 sprigs of rosemary, chopped

1 garlic clove, minced

6 cuts Akaushi beef tenderloin

1 cup of chicken stock

2 pounds of Brussels sprouts, trimmed and cleaned

2 teaspoons of salt,

Salt and pepper to taste

6 tablespoons of olive oil

6 cups of water

Directions

1. To prepare the Brussels sprouts, simply bring water, 2 teaspoons of salt and 2 tablespoons of olive oil to a boil. Add in the Brussels sprouts and cook the mixture for about 9 minutes. When tender, strain and set aside.

2. Then add in salt and pepper, the Brussels sprouts cut in half, and 2 tablespoons of olive oil into a sauté

287

pan. Cook on high heat until the sprouts are lightly brown and then add in the chicken stock and continue to cook until it steams.

3. To prepare the steaks, season them with salt and pepper. Add the olive oil that remained to a sauté pan. Heat over medium and then sear your steaks for 2 minutes or until the first side turns brown.

4. Stir the mixture and then add in minced rosemary and garlic. Lower the heat and continue to cook for 3-6 additional minutes or until done, while turning them occasionally. The cooking time for the steak depends on their thickness.

5. At this point, pour the juice from the meat over the Brussels sprouts, and then serve on the side of your tenderloin.

68: Oven-Roasted Bacon Veggies

Serves 4-6

Ingredients

Salt and pepper

Extra virgin olive oil

1/2 lb. of Brussels sprouts

3-4 zucchini

11 strips of bacon

For Balsamic Mustard Chicken

Salt and pepper to taste

2 ½ tablespoons of mustard, spicy brown

3 cloves of garlic, minced or chopped

¼ cup of extra virgin olive oil

¼ cup of Balsamic

2 chicken breasts, boneless and skinless

Directions

1. Rinse the chicken breasts, and put them on a chopping board. Use pepper and salt to season both

sides of the chicken breast and then transfer them into a zip lock bag.

2. Add in garlic, spicy brown mustard, extra virgin olive oil, and balsamic and then zip up the bag.

3. Massage your chicken while inside the bag and coat all sides with the spices. Cool the contents of the bag in the fridge and let marinate for at least 3 hours.

4. To cook the chicken, heat a medium-sized saucepan placed on medium heat and drizzle the pan with some extra virgin olive oil. Position the chicken breast on the pan and brown both sides.

5. Add in the marinade. Use a lid to cover and then allow the juices to reduce. Check and stir your chicken regularly to ensure it fully cooks. The pink skin color should fully disappear. If preferred, flip the skin once more until fully cooked.

6. At this point, prepare the "Oven Roasted Bacon Veggies" by cutting the bacon into small sizes and then frying until crispy. Set the cooked bacon on a plate lined with a paper towel to soak up the left over bacon grease and set them aside.

7. Clean the veggies and then cut the Brussels sprouts into half. Then on a cookie sheet lined with foil, place the sprouts and then slice the ends of the zucchini.

Also cut them into half lengthwise and then slice them into half-circle shapes.

8. Put the sliced zucchini on the cookie sheet that has the sprouts. Drizzle the mixture with sufficient amounts of olive oil, and then roast in the oven for 20-30 minutes at 350 degrees F.

9. When done, the mixture should turn a little brown and the Brussels sprouts tender. After about 20 minutes, add the bacon on the veggies so it can warm it.

10. To serve, sprinkle the veggies with salt and pepper.

Paleo Snack Recipes

69: Honey Roasted Carrots

Serves 4

Ingredients

1 teaspoon of fresh thyme or ½ teaspoon dried thyme

½ teaspoon of sea salt

1 tablespoon of raw honey

2 tablespoons of olive oil

1 large bunch of carrots, scrubbed

Directions

1. Preheat the oven to 425 degrees F. Meanwhile, use parchment paper to line a baking sheet.

2. Toss the carrots with thyme, salt, honey, and oil. Arrange the ingredients in an even layer and bake for 30 minutes.

3. Remove from the oven as soon as it has browned and caramelized, and let it cool for a moment. Serve and enjoy.

70: Coconut Flour Fudge Brownies

Makes 16 squares

Ingredients

3 large eggs

¼ cup of coconut flour

6 tablespoons butter, ghee or coconut oil, melted

1/4 teaspoon of salt

¾ cup of cacao powder, unsweetened

2 teaspoons of vanilla extract

¾ cup of maple syrup or honey

Directions

1. First, preheat the oven to 350 degrees F. Meanwhile, line the bottom of a baking pan with parchment paper.

2. Using a food processor, mixer, or a whisk, combine the flour, cocoa, salt and then add in vanilla, maple and eggs, and mix well to incorporate.

3. Let the batter sit for around 5 minutes. Then blend for a few more seconds.

4. Bake until ready or for about 25 minutes. To test whether the fudge is ready, just insert a toothpick into the brownies and check if it comes out clean.

5. Allow it to cool for a while to harden then slice the brownies. If necessary, allow them to rest for a few hours or overnight.

6. Serve or alternatively seal and store in the refrigerator for a few weeks. You can also store at room temperature for a few days.

71: Cinnamon Baked Apples

Servings: 4

Ingredients

1 cup apple juice

¼ cup of liquid honey, unpasteurized

4 apples

¼ teaspoon of ground cloves

½ teaspoon of nutmeg

1 teaspoon of cinnamon

1 teaspoon of grated fresh ginger root

2 dates, pitted and chopped

¼ cup of dried cranberries

½ cup of nuts and/or seeds

Directions

1. Preheat your oven to 325 degrees F and then combine spices, ginger root, dates, cranberries, nuts, and seeds in a bowl.

2. Core the apples; do not peel them because most of the nutrients and fiber are in the skin.

3. Stuff each apple with the seed and nut mixture and then drizzle some honey. Put in an 8 x 8 inch square baking dish.

4. Pour the cider around the apples to keep it moist, and then bake in the preheated oven for around 30-35 minutes.

5. As soon as the apples are soft, remove from the oven and serve.

72: Roasted Cauliflower with Bacon and Garlic

Serves 4

Ingredients

Sea salt and black pepper, freshly ground

2 teaspoons of olive oil

3 strips of bacon cut into bite sized pieces

6 garlic cloves, sliced thinly

1 head of cauliflower cut into small florets

Directions

1. Preheat oven to about 375 degrees F, as you toss together olive oil, bacon, garlic slices, and cauliflower on a baking sheet.

2. Roast the contents for about 20-25 minutes or until the cauliflower cooks through and the bacon is crisp.

3. Season the roasted cauliflower with salt and pepper to taste, and serve the snack.

73: Baked Cinnamon Apple Chips

Serves 1

Ingredients

1 teaspoon of cinnamon

1-2 apples

Directions

1. Preheat your oven to 200 degrees.

2. Use a sharp knife or mandolin to slice the apple into thin slices. Discard the seeds.

3. Line a baking sheet with parchment paper and arrange the apples on it, making sure they do not overlap. Once done, sprinkle cinnamon over the apples and then bake in the oven for 1 hour before flipping and cooking the other side for another hour. Continue baking and flipping until the apples turn crispy and are no longer moist. After, let cool, and then store in an airtight container

74: Raspberry Coconut Bark Fat Bombs

Serves 2

Ingredients

¼ cup of swerve sweetener, powdered

½ cup of shredded coconut, unsweetened

½ cup of coconut butter

½ cup of freeze-dried raspberries

½ cup of coconut oil

Directions

1. Use parchment paper to line an 8x8 inch pan and then set aside.

2. Blend dried berries in a food processor or coffee grinder to form a fine powder. Set aside.

3. Over medium heat, warm a small saucepan and then mix shredded coconut, coconut oil, coconut butter and the sweetener. Stir well to melt and incorporate.

4. Pour half of the batter into a baking pan and add raspberry powder to the remaining mixture in the pan. Stir well.

5. Dollop the raspberry mixture over the coconut mixture and then use a knife to swirl. Chill until set then break into chunks; Serve.

75: Candied Pecans

Serves 1

Ingredients

½ teaspoon of Celtic sea salt

2 tablespoons of sugar-free syrup

1 tablespoon of olive oil

2 cups of pecans

Directions

1. In a large bowl, toss the syrup, olive oil, pecans and Celtic sea salt, and then pour into a 9X13 inch baking dish.

2. Bake the mixture for around 15 minutes in a preheated oven at 350 degrees F.

3. Cool for a few minutes and then enjoy.

76: Paleo Sautéed Kale

Serves 1

Ingredients

Olive oil to coat pan

Sea salt

1 tablespoon of apple cider vinegar

¼ teaspoon of red pepper flakes

½-1 tablespoon of minced garlic

2 bunches of kale

Directions

1. In a large skillet, heat olive oil and then add the rest of the ingredients.

2. Cook the mixture over medium heat for about 3 to 5 minutes while stirring.

3. Serve and enjoy.

77: Cucumber Noodles with Blueberries

Serves: 6-8

Ingredients

1 cup of cilantro leaves

2 cups of blueberries

¼ cup of extra virgin olive oil

¼ teaspoon of cumin, ground

1 clove of garlic, finely chopped

4 teaspoons of lime juice, fresh

2 large jalapeño chilies, seeded and finely chopped

4 large cucumbers

Salt

Directions

1. Use a julienne peeler to prepare cucumber noodles.

2. Mix olive oil, cumin, garlic, lime juice, and jalapeno in a large bowl.

3. Add in cilantro, blueberries, and cucumber noodles and toss to coat.

78: Cherry Vanilla Power Bars

Serves 12

Ingredients

2-3 tablespoons of water

10 drops of vanilla crème stevia

1/3 cup of cranberries, dried

2/3 cup of dried cherries

1/3 cup of golden flax meal

2 ½ cups of slivered almonds

Directions

1. Put stevia, cranberries, cherries, flax meal, and the almonds in a food processor and pulse until smooth.

2. Pulse in the water to obtain a mixture resembling a ball.

3. Remove from the processor and press the mixture in an 8 x 8 inch baking dish.

4. Then slice the vanilla bars and serve.

79: Rosemary Sweet Potato Chips

Serves 10

Ingredients

Salt & pepper to taste

2 sweet potatoes

2 tablespoons of coconut oil

Directions

1. Preheat your oven to 400 degrees F.

2. Use a sharp knife to slice your sweet potatoes to bite-size pieces and then toss together with coconut oil. Ensure you rub the sweet potatoes fully in oil to coat.

3. Use parchment paper to line your baking sheet and then arrange your sweet potatoes on it.

4. Add salt, pepper, and rosemary to season and bake in the preheated oven for 25-30 minutes. To ensure they bake well with crispier texture, flip the potatoes once.

5. Once crispy brown with soft centers, remove from heat and let them chill to harden.

80: Paleo Asparagus Bundles

Serves 4

Ingredients

½ cup of fresh thyme or ¼ cup of thyme blossoms

2 tablespoons of fresh lemon juice

2 tablespoons of grated lemon peel

2 tablespoons of avocado butter

8 green onion stems

1 ½ pounds of asparagus, trimmed

Directions

1. Start by steaming the asparagus along with green onions in a steamer until crisp-tender.

2. Drain and divide the asparagus into 4 bundles. Tie each of the four bundles using two onion stems.

3. Transfer the bundles to a serving plate.

4. Combine avocado butter, lemon juice, lemon peel, and fresh thyme in a small bowl and then spoon it over the asparagus.

5. Garnish with lemon slices and remaining thyme.

81: Blueberry Coconut Popsicles

Serves: 10

Ingredients

2-3 tablespoons of pure maple syrup

3 cups of fresh blueberries

1 can of full-fat coconut milk

Directions

1. Add maple syrup, blueberries, and coconut milk to a blender and process until smooth. Scrape down the sides of the food processor as required.

2. Move the mixture into a Popsicle mold leaving around ¼-inch space at the top of the mold to help the popsicles expand in the freezer.

3. Follow the mold directions to insert the Popsicle sticks into the mold and then freeze the popsicle for about 6 to 8 hours.

4. When hard enough, remove from the freezer, and then let thaw for 1-2 minutes. If need be, you can run the mold under lukewarm water to loosen the popsicles.

5. Put the popsicle mold on flat surface and gently wiggle the snack out. Serve!

82: Crispy Kale Chips

Serves: 8

Ingredients

2 tablespoons of filtered water

½ teaspoon of gray sea salt or pink rock salt

1 tablespoon of raw honey

2 tablespoons of nutritional yeast

1 lemon, juiced

1 cup sweet potato, grated

1 cup fresh cashews, soaked for 2 hours

2 bunches of green curly kales cut into bite sizes

Directions

1. Run all the ingredients apart from kale in a food processor or blender until smooth.

2. Put kale in a large mixing bowl and then pour the blended ingredients over it. Use your hands to combine and coat the kale fully.

3. Transfer the kale onto parchment paper, and then set the oven to 150 degrees to dehydrate the kales for 2 hours.

4. Turn the leaves at some point to ensure smooth drying. Once done, remove from the oven and keep in an airtight container.

83: Kohlrabi-Carrot-Carpaccio

Serves 2

Ingredients

2 tablespoon of watercress

Salt & pepper

2 tablespoon of chives, fresh

½ lemon, juiced

1 celery root

1 spring onion

2 Kohlrabis

1 carrot

3 tablespoon of extra-virgin olive oil

Directions

1. Peel and dice the carrot, celery and spring onion.

2. Put the mixture in a salad bowl and incorporate the ingredients well.

3. Combine the watercress, chives, pepper, salt and lemon juice, together with the veggies in the bowl.

4. Then peel the kohlrabi, slice it into pieces, and then arrange them onto 2 big plates.

5. Pour the dressing-mix over the pieces and serve.

84: Paleo Pumpkin Bars

Yields 16 squares

Ingredients

½ cup of chocolate chunks

¼ cup of coconut oil

⅓ cup of organic honey

1 cup of roasted pumpkin, fresh

4 large eggs

½ teaspoon of cinnamon

½ teaspoon of baking soda

¼ teaspoon of Celtic sea salt

⅓ cup of coconut flour

Directions

1. Combine cinnamon, baking soda, salt and coconut floor in a food processor and then pulse in oil, honey, pumpkin, and eggs until fully mixed.

2. Stir in the chocolate chips by hand and transfer the batter into a baking dish measuring 8 x 8 inch.

3. Bake the contents in an oven at 350 degrees F for around 20-30 minutes.

4. When ready or fully cooked through, cool and then serve.

85: Guacamole with Tomatoes

Serves: 4

Ingredients

1 pinch of cayenne pepper, ground

1 clove of garlic, minced

2 plum tomatoes, diced

Handful of fresh coriander, chopped

½ onion, diced

1 teaspoon of salt

1 lime, juiced

3 avocados, peeled, stones removed and mashed

Directions

1. Mash together avocados, salt and lime juice in a medium bowl.

2. Then add in garlic, tomatoes, coriander, and onion. Now stir in cayenne pepper.

3. Serve the snack immediately or refrigerate for an hour for extra flavor.

86: Barbecue Zucchini Chips

Serves: 6-8

Ingredients

Olive oil

3 zucchinis

½ teaspoon of black pepper

½ teaspoon of mustard

½ teaspoon of cumin

1 teaspoon of paprika

1 teaspoon of garlic powder

1 tablespoon of sea salt

1-2 tablespoon of coconut sugar, sweetener

1 tablespoon of chili powder

Directions

1. Preheat your oven to 300 degrees F.

2. In a small bowl, combine cayenne, black pepper, mustard, cumin, paprika, garlic, sea salt, coconut sugar, and chili powder to prepare a barbecue spice blend.

3. Slice the zucchini to make 1/8 inch slices and mist the olive oil over the zucchini slices. Now sprinkle the spice blend over the slices of zucchini and bake for about 40 minutes.

4. Once cooked through, remove the slices from the oven, flip them, and mist some olive oil on the other side. Sprinkle the spice blend over the sprinkled side too.

5. Bake for around 20 minutes but take care not to over-bake the chips.

87: Cilantro Lime Paleo Hummus

Serves 1

Ingredients

Salt to taste

½ cup of fresh cilantro

1 teaspoon of garlic powder, roasted

Juice of 2 limes

¼ cup of extra virgin olive oil

2 zucchini, peeled and chopped

Directions

1. In a food processor, add tahini and zucchini, and then process to combine fully.

2. Add in the other ingredients apart from the salt and cilantro and then process. Add in the cilantro and then season with salt.

88: Coconut Date Bars

Serves 4

Ingredients

1 teaspoon of coconut oil

¼ cup of cashews, or to taste

10 pitted dates, or to taste

½ cup of flaked coconut

1/3 cup of slivered almonds

Directions

1. In a food processor, blend coconut and almonds, then add dates. Pulse the mixture to incorporate.

2. Add in coconut oil and the cashews, and continue to pulse to obtain a thick sticky mixture.

3. Pour the mixture onto waxed paper. Make into a square by folding the sides of the paper over the top.

4. Put into the fridge for 30-60 minutes until chilled and solid.

89: Delightful Dates

Serves 12

Ingredients

½ teaspoon of cinnamon

1 cup of water

1 cup of pitted dates

Directions

1. Place the dates in a small saucepan, and then pour water over them until completely covered.

2. Over high heat, bring the water to a boil then lower the heat to low. Simmer until the dates are soft and broken down, in about 45-60 minutes.

3. Remove from heat and let it cool for around 15 minutes.

4. Transfer the mixture along with the liquid into a food processor or blender and puree until smooth consistency.

5. At this point, sprinkle cinnamon and stir. Serve or keep chilled in a sealed container.

90: Buttered Brussels Sprouts

Serves 4

Ingredients

Black pepper, freshly ground

½ teaspoon of salt

Juice from ½ lemon

¼ ghee, melted

1.1 lb. of Brussels sprouts

Optional

¼ cup of toasted flaked almonds

¼ cup of toasted cashew nuts

¼ cup of toasted pine nuts

1 medium white onion, sliced

2 cloves garlic, crushed

½ cup soaked dried porcini mushrooms

Directions

1. Preheat your oven to 400 degrees F. Halve or quarter the Brussels sprouts and then pour melted ghee over them.

2. Drizzle with lemon juice and season with pepper and salt. Combine well.

3. Bake until crispy on the outside and tender inside, for about 25-35 minutes.

4. Mix a couple of times to ensure even cooking. Serve and enjoy.

91: Almond Butter Chocolate Milkshake

Serve 1

Ingredients

5 drops of stevia

1 tablespoon of almond butter, unsweetened

1 tablespoon of cocoa powder, unsweetened

1 cup of unsweetened coconut milk

Dash of sea salt

Directions

1. Blend all the ingredients until frothy.

2. Pour into a glass and enjoy.

92: Almond Butter Bites

Serves: 6-8

Ingredients

¼ teaspoon of cinnamon

2 tablespoons of shredded coconut, unsweetened

¼ cup of chopped almonds

¼ cup of raisins

¼ cup of raw sunflower seeds

½ cup of almond butter

Directions

1. In a bowl, mix all the ingredients until well incorporated.

2. Using a large melon ball scoop or ½ tablespoon measuring spoon, scoop the mixture to create small balls.

3. Put the balls in an 8x8 inch baking dish and freeze to firm up.

4. Serve chilled or slightly thawed.

93: Apple & Bacon Stuffed Pork Chops

Serves 4

Ingredients

½ teaspoon of pepper

1 tablespoon of salt

1 tablespoon of lemon juice

¼ teaspoon of paprika

4 fresh sage leaves, finely chopped

2 cloves of garlic, minced

1 red onion, diced

10 strips of bacon, diced

2 medium baking apples, peeled, cored and diced

2 tablespoon of lard

6 1-inch thick pork chops

Directions

1. To prepare the chops, pick a 4-6 inch knife and then pierce the fatty side of your chop. Now wiggle the knife side to side to make the pocket take up 70% of the chop.

2. In a cast iron skillet or medium pan, melt lard over medium heat and then cook together the onion, bacon, and the apples until softened. The bacon should turn crispy in about 8 minutes.

3. Add in lemon juice, paprika, sage and garlic, and toss for about 2 minutes. When done, remove the mixture from heat, move into a bowl, and then set aside.

4. To each pork chop, add salt and pepper, and then stuff with enough stuffing. To close or to prevent any spilling of stuffing, just use a toothpick or a skewer.

5. Insert the pork chops into the hot pan and then cook each of the sides for 5 minutes over medium-high heat.

6. Bake the contents of the pan in an oven at 350 degree F uncovered for about 35 minutes.

7. To serve the chops, simply warm the remaining stuffing, and then spoon the stuffing on each of your chops.

Paleo Dessert Recipes

94: Greek Tart with Apricot Jam

Serves 6-8

Ingredients:

300 grams of apricot jam

2 teaspoons of homemade baking powder (shown below-do not use store bought)

2 eggs

¾ cup of coconut sugar

500 grams of almond flour

280 grams of coconut butter

Directions

1. Use a mixer to whisk butter and then add in eggs and the coconut sugar. Add in the flour gradually until you make a soft dough. Place the dough in the fridge for around 30 minutes.

2. Once chilled for 30 minutes, roll out 2/3 of the dough in a greased or buttered tart pan, placing it all around the pan sides. Press it gently to evenly cover and join with the bottom.

3. Roll out the extra dough 1/2cm thick and then cut it into strips.

4. Evenly spread the apricot jam and then cover the dough strips. Now bake it at 180 degrees F for 45 minutes.

95: Sugar-Free Chocolate Pie

Serves 20

Ingredients

¼ teaspoon of salt

1 teaspoon of baking soda

1 cup of all-purpose flour

½ cup of chopped walnuts

1 teaspoon of vanilla extract

2 eggs

½ cup of ghee

1 cup of water

½ cup of chopped raisins

½ cup of pitted prunes

½ cup of pitted dates

Directions

1. Cut the prunes and dates into small pieces. Then boil water, raisins, prunes, and dates for 5 minutes.

2. Once ready, add in ghee, mix, and set aside to cool down. Meanwhile, preheat the oven to 350 degrees F.

3. Mix the nuts, vanilla and eggs, and add to the fruit mixture. Then sift the flour, salt and baking soda, and add to the fruit mixture.

4. You can add ¼ teaspoon of nutmeg and ½ teaspoon of cinnamon for a spicy bar. Spread the batter in a 7x11 inch pan and bake for about 30 minutes.

96: Almond and Coconut Muffin

Serves 1

Ingredients

1 teaspoon of extra virgin olive oil

1 large egg

1/8 teaspoon of salt

¼ teaspoon of baking powder

½ teaspoon of cinnamon

1 teaspoon of sucralose based sweetener

1/3 tablespoon of organic coconut flour, high fiber

2 tablespoon of almond meal flour

Directions

1. Add all the dry ingredients to a coffee mug and stir to incorporate.

2. Add in oil and egg, and mix well.

3. Microwave for about 60 seconds then use a knife to remove the muffin from the cup.

4. Slice, and serve.

97: Turmeric Chia Pudding

Serves: 2-4

Ingredients

⅛ teaspoon of ground cloves

⅛ teaspoon of ground cardamom

½ teaspoon of cinnamon

1 teaspoon of ground turmeric

2 tablespoon of maple syrup

⅓ cup of chia seeds

1½ cups of cashew milk or almond milk

Directions

1. Combine all the above ingredients in a bowl.

2. Pour the mixture into individual jars or bowls then let set overnight.

3. Eat the pudding plain or top with nuts and fruits.

98: Beet Chocolate Pudding

Serves: 4

Ingredients

1/8 teaspoon of sea salt

½ teaspoon of ground cinnamon

1/3 cup of pure maple syrup

½ cup of full-fat canned coconut milk

½ cup of red beet roasted

½ cup of unsweetened cocoa powder or raw cacao powder

2 large ripe avocados peeled and diced

Directions

1. Add all the ingredients to a food processor and process to obtain a smooth mixture.

2. At some point while processing, stop the blender a couple of times to scrap the sides then re-start again to get a smoother consistency.

3. Move the pudding to a sealable container and keep it chilled for a few hours. Serve it with coconut whipped cream.

99: Paleo Angel Food Cake

Serves: 12

Ingredients

12 large egg whites at room temperature

1 pint of berries, optional

1¼ teaspoon of cream of tartar

1½ cups of whipped coconut cream

¾ cup of coconut or maple sugar

1 teaspoon of fresh lemon juice

1 tablespoon of pure vanilla extract

¼ teaspoon of Celtic salt

1 cup of arrowroot flour

Directions

1. Preheat the oven to 350 degrees F and move the rack to the middle position.

2. Using a stand mixer, whisk together the egg whites and lemon juice on medium-high for 30 seconds or until the mixture gets foamy. Add in salt, cream of tartar, vanilla, and whisk on medium-high for 1-2 minutes or until soft peaks form.

3. With the mixer still on medium-high, slowly add in the ½ cup of maple sugar a tablespoon at a time.

4. Sift the remaining ¼ cup of arrowroot flour and maple sugar into a small bowl. Turn the mixer to medium and then slowly add in the arrowroot mixture. Turn the speed back to medium-high and whip to smoothness. You are likely to note tiny lumps caused by the sugar; these will melt once the cake starts baking.

5. Pour the batter into a non-oiled clean, 12-cup angel food cake pan; bake for 40-45 minutes or until the cake looks puffed and the top starts turning golden brown. Remove from the oven and then turn the cake upside down. Let the cake cool for 1 hour or more and then after, use a knife—by running it outside of the cake—to invert the cake onto a platter

100: Paleo Lemon Bars

Serves: 9-12 bars

Ingredients

For the crust:

¼ teaspoon of sea salt

1 cup of almond floor

1 teaspoon of vanilla

1 tablespoon of honey

½ tablespoon of Paleo-friendly baking soda

¼ cup of almond butter

1 tablespoon of coconut oil

For the filling:

A pinch of salt

2 ½ tablespoons of coconut flour

½ cup of honey

¼ cup of lemon juice

3 eggs

1 tablespoon of finely grated lemon zest

Directions

1. Preheat the oven to 350 degrees F. Use the coconut oil to coat a 9x9 baking dish.

2. Use a food processor to combine all the crust ingredients into a crumble. Once formed, press it into the bottom of the pan, use a fork to prick several holes into the crust, and then bake for 10 minutes.

3. Meanwhile, use a food processor to combine all the filling ingredients until well incorporated. Once crust is done, remove from oven and evenly pour the filling over the top. Return to the oven and bake for an additional 15-20 minutes or until the filling sets but can still jiggle a little.

4. Transfer to a wire rack and let cool completely. If preferred, you can chill in the fridge.

101: Chocolate Hot Cross Buns

Serves: 8

Ingredients

¼ cup of sultanas (golden raisins)

½ teaspoon of bicarb soda

1½ tablespoons of coconut flour

2 egg whites

¼ cup of cacao powder

½ cup of coconut flour

¼ orange juice

¼ cup of honey

½ cup of coconut milk

4 eggs

Directions

1. Preheat the oven to 340 degrees F and use coconut oil to grease 8 muffin tins.

2. Use an electric beater to beat the eggs for a minute; add in honey, orange juice, and coconut milk then beat for a few seconds more.

3. Add in the cacao powder, bicarb soda, and coconut flour and combine with electric beater for one minute.

4. Stir in the sultanas and then scoop the batter into the muffin tins.

5. Use your electric beater to beat the eggs and then add coconut floor. Beat the mixture again.

6. Scoop the eggs mixture into plastic bag, snip off the corner and now pipe onto the top of buns to make crosses. Bake the buns for around 17-20 minutes before serving.

102: Banana Bread Bars with Chocolate Chips

Serves 1 bar

Ingredients

1 medium zucchini, shredded

1/8 teaspoon of sea salt

2 eggs

¾ cup of cashew butter

½ teaspoon of cinnamon

2 tablespoons of pure maple syrup

2 medium-sized ripe bananas, mashed

1/3 cup of dairy-free, Paleo friendly chocolate chips (optional)

½ teaspoon of baking soda

1 teaspoon of vanilla extract

½ cup of coconut flour

For topping

1 teaspoon of coconut oil

2 tablespoons of dairy-free, Paleo-friendly chocolate chips (optional)

Directions

1. Preheat your oven to 350 degrees F. Use parchment paper to line a 9X9 inch pan and spray with nonstick cooking spray—this will keep the sides from sticking.

2. In a large bowl, mix the zucchini, banana, cashew butter, maple syrup, eggs, and the vanilla until well combined and smooth. Add the coconut flour, cinnamon, baking soda, and salt to taste and stir to mix the dry and wet ingredients. Fold in 1/3 cup chocolate chips if using.

3. Pour the mixture into the prepared pan and bake for 30-40 minutes—when you prick the bars with a toothpick, it should come out clean.

3. Transfer the bars to a wire rack and let cool. For the chocolate drizzle topping, mix chocolate chips and coconut oil in small saucepan and then place the saucepan over low heat. Stir frequently as the mixture melts and then once melted, drizzle over the bars.

103: Pecan Hotcakes with Mixed Berries

Serves 10

Ingredients

Organic oil

Warmed frozen berries

¼ teaspoon of pure liquid stevia

½ teaspoon of baking soda

½ teaspoon of cinnamon, ground

2 teaspoons of pure vanilla extract

4 whole eggs

8 ounces of raw pecan pieces

Directions:

1. Pulse your pecans in a food processor or blender to obtain a fine pecan meal. Pour the pecans into a large mixing bowl and then whisk together with stevia, baking soda, cinnamon, vanilla, and eggs.

2. Warm some oil in a pan and then ladle about 2 tablespoons of batter in the pan. Cook the pancake until light and fluffy on both sides. Your hotcakes should fluff up when cooking.

3. Use a microwave or pot to warm the frozen berries and then ladle them onto your hotcakes and serve.

104: Mango-Peach Popsicles

Serves 10

Ingredients

Juice from a 1/2 orange

3 ripe peaches

3 ripe mangoes

Directions

1. Peel your peaches and mangoes and then cut the peeled fruit.

2. Place them in a processor and squeeze in half an orange. Blend to a smooth consistency.

3. At this point, spoon the mixture into Popsicle molds, and then freeze.

105: Fried Honey Bananas

Serves 1

Ingredients

Olive oil or coconut oil

Cinnamon to taste

1 tablespoon of organic honey

1 banana, sliced

Directions

1. Lightly drizzle oil in a skillet placed over medium heat.

2. Then arrange banana slices in the skillet and cook for around 1-2 minutes on each side.

3. As the banana slices cook, whisk a tablespoon of water and organic honey.

4. Remove the slices from heat, pour your honey mixture over the sliced cooked bananas, and let cool.

4. Once cooled, sprinkle with cinnamon and serve.

106: Chocolate Paleo Brownie

Serves 1

Ingredients

1 teaspoon of vegan chocolate chips

2 teaspoons of cocoa powder

1 teaspoon of coconut flour

1 teaspoon of coconut oil, softened

1 egg white

3 tablespoons of almond meal

1-2 inch banana, mashed

1 tablespoon of almond milk, unsweetened

Directions

1. Preheat your oven to 350 degrees F.

2. Spray a ramekin or a small baking dish with non-stick cooking spray and set aside.

3. In a medium sized bowl, smash a banana and then add in eggs white, almond milk, coconut oil, and mix.

4. Combine until the texture of the contents resembles the typical brownie batter.

5. Pour the batter in a baking dish and bake in the preheated oven until the middle is well cooked. This should take about 22-25 minutes.

107: Healthy Dark Chocolate

Makes 100 grams

Ingredients

Seeds of 1 vanilla bean

2½ tablespoons of cocoa powder

1½ tablespoon of maple syrup

3½ tablespoons of cocoa butter

Directions

1. Over low heat, melt cocoa butter in a small saucepan and then stir in vanilla bean seeds, cocoa powder, and maple syrup. Whisk the mixture until smooth.

2. Check the chocolate's temperature using a candy thermometer. Heat to 120 degrees F and then cool in the fridge at 79 degrees F for 10-15 minutes. Ensure you stir the contents every 5 minutes.

3. Once the time elapses, remove from the fridge and heat at a constant temperature of 87 degrees F.

4. Pour into the mold, cool, and then refrigerate the chocolate until ready to serve.

108: Paleo Strawberry Crumble

Serves 4

Ingredients

¼ teaspoon of vanilla bean paste

500g of strawberries

5 fresh pitted medjool dates

½ teaspoon of cinnamon, ground

40g of pistachio nut

40g of almonds

Directions

1. In a food processor, mix cinnamon, pistachio and almonds, and puree to obtain a crumble-like consistency. You can also chop by hand if you don't have a blender.

2. In a powerful blender, blend half of the strawberries, 2 fresh dates and vanilla until well blended.

3. Cut the remaining strawberries into quarters. Mix the blended puree and the quartered strawberries.

4. Divide the contents into serving bowls and then serve with the crumble topping.

109: Macadamia Almond Cream

Serves 2-4

Ingredients

2 lb. fresh cherries

1 teaspoon of stevia

Fresh cherries

1 tablespoon of vanilla powder

2 cups of fresh almond milk

2 oz. almonds

10 oz. macadamia nuts

Directions

1. Soak the almonds and macadamia nuts in distilled or alkaline water overnight or for at least 12 hours.

2. Blend the soaked nuts together with vanilla powder, almond milk, and Stevia to create a fine and smooth paste.

3. Refrigerate the mixture for around 3 hours before serving with fresh cherries.

110: Guilt-Free Banana Pudding

Serves 4

Ingredients

1 ripe banana, sliced

¼ cup of arrowroot powder

4 egg yolks

2 cups of full-fat coconut milk

¼ cup of honey

½ teaspoon of salt

1 teaspoon of vanilla extract

2 ripe bananas, mashed

Walnuts (optional)

Directions

1. In a medium-sized glass bowl, whisk the egg yolks, honey, and arrowroot powder and then set aside.

2. Use a small saucepan placed over medium-high heat to heat the coconut milk for 5 minutes as you stir occasionally. Pour the coconut mixture into the egg mixture while whisking constantly.

3. Transfer the mixture to the saucepan and cook for 2-3 minutes while stirring regularly until the mixture thickens—ensure it does not boil.

4. Drain the mixture into a large bowl and whisk in the vanilla and mashed bananas. Chill for at least an hour.

5. To serve, spoon the pudding into a glass and top with bananas and walnuts if using. Serve immediately.

111: Pressure Cooker Pumpkin Pie

Serves 6-8

Ingredients

For Crust

2 tablespoons of coconut butter

1/3 cup of toasted pecans, chopped

6 crushed Pecan Sandies cookies

For filling

½ cup of almond or coconut milk

1½ cups of solid pack pumpkin

1 egg, beaten

1½ teaspoon of pumpkin pie spice

½ teaspoon of salt

½ cup of coconut sugar

Directions

1. Coat a 7-inch spring-form pan with non-stick cooking spray and then combine coconut butter, chopped pecans, and cookie crumbs into a bowl.

2. Spread the batter evenly at the bottom and about an inch up the side of the pan and put into a freezer for 10 minutes.

3. To make the filling, mix together pumpkin pie spice, salt and sugar into a large bowl and then whisk in pumpkin, egg, and the milk.

4. Pour the batter into the piecrust and use aluminum foil to cover the top of your spring-form.

5. Add a cup of water to the cooker's pot and position the trivet at the bottom. Center the filled pan carefully on a foil sling and drop it into the cooking pot.

6. Fold the foil sling in order to prevent any interruption with the lid closing. Once set, lock the lid in place.

7. Cook for 35 minutes with pressure set to high and then turn off the cooker after you hear a beep sound.

8. Release the pressure and wait for the valve to drop before you remove the lid. Take out the pie and see whether the middle has set and if not, cook for another 5 minutes.

9. Remove the spring-form pan to a wire rack in order to cool, and remove the aluminum foil.

10. Once the pie has cooled fully, cover it with plastic wrap and keep refrigerated for more than 4 hours.

Conclusion

We have come to the end of the book. Thank you for reading and congratulations for reading until the end.

The Paleo diet is very effective for weight loss and optimal health so you shouldn't find it hard to give up on carbs, especially wheat, grains and starchy food. Instead of paying attention to those foods you're going to give up, why don't you just focus on the healthy alternatives that you will get to enjoy while on the diet? It's my hope that this book has been very informative if not motivational as far as Paleo dieting is concerned. Now it's your time to go out there and fully adopt the caveman diet!

Finally, if you enjoyed this book, then I'd like to ask you a favor. Would you be kind enough to leave a review for this book on Amazon, please? I would greatly appreciate receiving your reviews!

I love getting feedback from my customers and reviews on Amazon. Your reviews really DO make a difference. If I get more good reviews, I will be able to publish more books. I read all my reviews and would really appreciate your thoughts.

Go here to leave a review for this book on Amazon!

amzn.to/2MOVwtA

Check Out Our Other Books

Below you'll find some of our other books that are popular on Amazon and Kindle as well.

Go to the link below

https://amzn.to/2l2QsFg

If the links do not work, for whatever reason, you can simply search for these titles on the Amazon website to find them.